Life is good!

OLD MEN DREAM

by Pete Fullerton

Love,

Pete Fullerton

Additional information or copies may be obtained by writing:

Truck of Love
P.O. Box 269
Los Altos, CA 94023

www.truckoflove.org
or
peteandsue@netgate.net

Dedication

This book is dedicated to my most amazing family.

To my wife, Sue

To my children and their spouses

To my grandchildren

Tim, Julie, Ian, Peter, Andy, Lonie, Robba, Katrine, Kerri, Gregory, Kayleigh, Timothy, Samantha, Anthony, Alissa, Ethan, and Ella

I love you!

Acknowledgments

I would like to thank all who helped me in this transcription of *Old Men Dream*.

First on my list of thanks is Pam Lehner; for her relentless typing and her great input on structuring my thoughts. Pam, you are a blessing.

Secondly, I would like to thank Lisa Walter for transcribing my notes about some dreams that occurred before my journey. Neither Lisa nor I knew these dreams would become reality.

Also, thanks to my wife, Sue, and my children: Tim, Julie, Ian, Peter and Andy. The difficult decisions seem to be made by those closest to me. I thank you and love you all.

If there is anything to be learned by the recording of this journey, I leave it up to you.

Shalom,

P.F.

12/17/07

Foreword

My love for the poor and helpless began early in my life. My first ministry began when I was four years old and my grandmother told me that healthy dogs had wet noses and that sick dogs had dry noses. I went all over my neighborhood looking for dogs with dry noses. Then I would lick their noses to make them well. Although this ministry didn't last very long, I knew I had done what was right because these dogs thanked me by licking my face! (I realize this is a child's point of view, but it was a true act of love.)

My next foray into charitable works came when I was eleven. I offered rides in my wagon for two cents. After a day of hard work pulling the neighborhood kids up and down Saint Bonaventure Street, I had $2.00 that I donated to the Crippled Children's Fund. Gail Abernathy and I even got our pictures in the town paper!

As a child I loved spending time with the homeless. In those days they were known as hobos. Down at the railroad tracks I heard these men tell lots of stories. I had no idea this would be my story in forty more years.

After the normal growing up years (when I explored all sorts of interests—some good—some not-so-good), I became interested in music and even toured in the 60's with a band known as "We Five."

Marriage to Sue came along and with that arrived five children. As my family grew I found that old time yearning to work with the poor and so in 1986 I entered full time ministry with the poor through my own not-for-profit corporation known locally as "Truck of Love." Sue and I have been committed together to helping people in need.

Truck of Love has involved twice yearly trips to the Arizona desert to deliver food and clothing to the poor. I have also spent my days working on the San Francisco Peninsula and San Jose area helping people who live on the street, in motels, shelters, or run-down apartments. From 1986–1996 Sue and I led trips with teens to Tijuana, Mexico. There we worked in several colonias where we conducted schools, built houses, and worked with some really wonderful people. In 1986 we also started a summer camp in the Arizona desert on the Tohono O'Odham Indian Reservation that serves about 160 children and adults each summer. But all that is another story—suffice it to say, I have been working with the poor for some years.

When I was called to this other ministry of being homeless all I had to do is say: "Yes!" There were plenty of comments from well-meaning friends that made me realize it was the time to take that leap of faith. There came a moment when I had to see the light and there was no turning back.

Of course the names and some identifying locations have been changed to allow those I met along the way maintain their privacy and security.

Introduction

This is a book of dreams. It began in a dream and unfolds as a dream—the dream of a lifetime. It is a mixture of dreams and people—some with names, some without. Each person has powerful and colorful stories. It is a book of events that happened as a result of having said "Yes!" to God. It was God who created in me through the dreams, the desire to walk among the forgotten poor who live on the streets of America. Each time on my journey when I came to a crossroads where I hesitated, I remembered those dreams given to me by God.

For many years I have written down my dreams. Because of a series of five dreams that began in May 1995, I chose to become homeless. We are all dreamers, but few of us ever act on our dreams. I took action on these dreams because I truly felt God speaking to me.

The dreams laid out a plan that I was to follow: I would be homeless for three months, I was to take nothing with me, I would meet my guardian or guardians (this wasn't clear to me), and I would leave on August 14, 1997 from a state other than my own (California being my home). The dreams gave me no other details.

I told my wife, Sue about the series of dreams. I wanted her opinion. I knew she would have an understanding beyond my own. I don't know what went through Sue's mind when I told her. Did she think I had completely and finally lost it? All I can say with certainty is that she is a beautiful woman who is literally half my physical size. Her inner beauty shines through when she talks and she always speaks the truth. I knew I could trust her voice.

Sue gave me her blessing. She could see that my desire to see these dreams to fruition was in the deepest spot of my soul. Her words to me were simple and to the point: "If this is what you are called to do, then follow your calling."

She told me to "follow my heart"—with a few amendments. She wanted me to go, but for two months, not three. (She is ever practical and worked out when I could be gone between the needs of our summer programs in Tijuana, Mexico and the summer day camp for the children of the Tohono O'Odham Nation in Arizona and the beginning of the local needs of the poor during the Thanksgiving and Christmas season. That meant I had a break from late August to late October.) She also told me I was to take $100.00 cash and some food. She said even homeless people have some cash. I've always loved the way Sue handles me with such gentleness. Only she can help me reason with the impulsive side of myself. Her firm but gentle reason prevailed.

Of course I couldn't begin this exploration without the consent of my children—all five of them. Again on Sue's advice, I waited until about six months before I was scheduled to begin my journey before I talked with our children. I approached them one by one. As expected, they each reacted differently. By this time in our family history they had seen me through many life changes and understood that I was probably going to do this anyway. My grandson, Gregory, who was ten years old at the time, had the most casual response. I took him out to breakfast and broke the news that I would be gone for two months. He didn't say anything until the waitress brought our food and then he asked: "Is that all you're getting Grandpa?" For him, it was life as usual.

Sue and I have learned that when God talks to us, we do what He asks. This attitude of surrender has come after years of prayer and discernment. We want to make sure it is God asking the questions and making the suggestions. When we attempt to follow God's will we discover many hidden blessings and that has made all the difference in our lives. No matter how hard life may become, we try to keep to the task at hand. Sue and I try to keep in mind a favorite quote from chapter six of The Book of Micah: "You have been told...what is good, and what the Lord requires of you: Only to do what is right, to love goodness and to walk humbly with your God." Thus began my journey as "Old Man."

PART
I

CHAPTER 1

We slept on the floor of our son and daughter-in-law's apartment the night of August 13. It was a restless night. I kept thinking how much I would miss my wife and family. Five a.m. came quickly. Sue and I rolled over toward each other and hugged quietly, holding on for the longest time. We dragged ourselves out of bed and off the floor. Sue made me a cup of coffee. She lit a candle and we prayed together for a few short minutes. She told me she would light a candle each day I was gone to keep me in prayer. It was time for me to go.

With nothing but a backpack and $80.00 in cash, I began my journey on August 14, 1997 from Ashland, Oregon. My dreams had told me I was to leave from a state other than California and it happened just so!

I placed a sign saying "NORTH" on the backpack and struggled to put it on. It held my life for the next two months: three sets of underwear, socks, and t-shirts, two pair of shorts, three outer t-shirts, one pair of dress pants and one dress shirt (in case I got work), one pair of jeans, one pair of new shoes, two sets of shoe strings, a first aide kit, one toothbrush, a shaving kit, two cans of deodorant, my blood pressure medication, a drawing pad, a writing pad, pencils, a rain poncho, eight plastic garbage bags (for dirty clothes and emergencies), signs (saying North, South, East, West), a dozen Cliff Bars, and two water bottles. I strapped my sleeping bag to the bottom. I had the cash in my left sock—just for safekeeping.

I opened the door of the apartment and with one last kiss I was on my way. I had now become "Old Man." My name came from the Bible passage in The Book of Joel: "...your old men shall dream dreams and your young men shall see visions."

5:30 A.M. The Goodbye

CHAPTER 2

My heart was filled with love for life and an excitement for the mystery about to unfold. My spirit was on fire. This was going to be a completely new experience. I knew I would make discoveries about myself, my world and the people surrounding me.

My name, Old Man, was important for several reasons. I didn't want to be identified. I knew from my experience working with street people that I was not the ordinary homeless person. I really didn't want to call attention to myself. (Of course I was carrying about 260 pounds on my frame so I was bound to attract some attention!) I needed to fall into a role much like an actor and changing my name helped remind me of my reasons for doing this. I wanted to relate more clearly with my homeless brothers and sisters.

Attuned to every second, to every sense, I walked from my son, Tim's, cozy apartment and Sue's embrace, up the street toward the freeway. The road I saw before me was full of promise. The wakening sounds of morning were accented; the different fragrances from cars and flowers were delicious aromas. The backpack and my shoes were still light upon my body. I could almost taste the morning. My mood was completely happy. I knew this was a wonderful place—physically and spiritually. I thought that if Sue and the family knew how much fun I was having, they would certainly have joined my sojourn. Already I looked forward to the promised weekly phone conversation with Sue. (That was one more stipulation she made—just to know I was "safe.")

Within fifteen minutes of setting out a blue and white VW van stopped to pick me up. "Need a ride?" the young man asked.

My simple "Yes!" began the real journey.

The driver was a pleasant-looking fellow with wiry blond hair bushed out into a "fro." The combination of his bright shirt and khaki pants let me know he was single and dressed himself. (Sue would never let me out in public looking like that! Well, she tries not to.) For several minutes he just drove and nothing was said. I opened the window to enjoy the smell of the wild flowers and the scent of ripening berries growing next to the highway. Being the passenger in a slow moving VW bus, there were many wonders to be seen that would have been missed at a higher speed. The sound of the meadowlark singing, the whisper of the wind and the smell of the fragrant pine trees created a precious moment on this first morning. I could see the sun's rays pop through the trees like bright notes on a page of music. I wanted to sing. I told myself that from this moment on, nothing would go unnoticed.

After a long silence (when I was recalling some long-ago memories of childhood), the young man said, "I like the sign on your back. Where are you headed anyway?"

I answered, "North."

The driver gave a little chuckle and said he knew that from my sign! As I came back to my surroundings, I told him I was going to Portland.

"And after that?" he asked.

"Well I'll probably be heading east tomorrow. I just don't know and I don't much care."

The conversation from then on was filled with good-hearted humor and male bonding. The young man confided in me that he was born into a wealthy family. He was beating a hasty retreat from a domineering mother and an absentee father who was a doctor somewhere on the east coast. He and I shared a love of the performing arts, which gave us plenty of common ground for conversation. He had just attended several performances at the Shakespeare Festival. He loved what he had seen. Of course I couldn't resist.

"Did you see *As You Like It?*" I asked.

"Oh, yes, it was one of my favorites. How about you?" he responded.

I smiled as I answered, "My son was in that particular play. He had a small part in a singing ensemble. He loves to act and is hoping to receive larger parts as time goes on. I'm very proud of him."

The young man said he remembered enjoying the ensemble singers as well as the madrigals. It was amazing how two strangers can find so much to talk about and how quickly connections can be made. He finally introduced himself to me as Fred. I responded that I was Old Man. With that Fred began to dump the bucket of his life.

Every few minutes he would check to see if I was truly listening and ask me what I thought. Sometimes I would have to ask him to repeat what he had just said, but mostly I seemed to pass his criteria as a person who would listen. His story was interesting and at times it was inspired by real passion in his telling.

He was 23 years old and a college graduate. He was the son of parents who each had full-time professions. His father was a doctor and his mother a lawyer. They had supported him financially all his life. They had definite ideas about what they wanted him to do. He had dreams of a life much different than the ideas expressed by his parents.

When several moments of quiet eventually passed, Fred asked if I would like to listen to music. Once or twice he would notice the expression on my face and would ask what I was thinking. To one of these queries I responded, "I'm not thinking, I'm remembering some stuff from past times."

Then, trying to drive the conversation a little deeper, I asked, "What was the happiest time in your life?"

He thought a few seconds before he glanced my way with a wry, impish grin. "Well," he said, "I suppose it was the day before yesterday, when I got away from the house—away from my Mom and the thought of my Dad who has never been there for me."

"Really?" I asked. "That was your happiest day?"

"Yeah," said Fred. "I can't think of a single happier time than the moment I stood face-to-face with my Mom and told her I wasn't going to live at home any more." As I sat in silence, he continued. "Everything I grew up with, all the religion crammed down my throat, all the control issues my parents had concerning me—was junk. I knew it and so did they." Fred finished his thought by saying, "Now it's time to dump it all and think for myself."

Sue and I had listened to hundreds of teenagers over the years through our parish youth ministry. At the risk of alienating him, I had to ask: "Fred, did you dump the gifts they gave you as well?"

"What gifts?" he asked.

"Oh, the gifts like this car we're riding in, the clothes on your back or the money in your bank account?"

"No," said Fred in a matter-of-fact way. "This van is a going away gift from them. They told me to take the money in my bank account. I think deep down in their hearts they both think I'm coming back, but I'm not!"

Fortunately, he didn't throw me out of the van as a result of my question. I thought I would try to sensor my comments before trying one like that again. But I also felt it was my duty to help

Fred look a little deeper into his thinking. For now the inter-change had given us plenty to think about and for a long time we were each lost in our own thoughts. I was lulled into sleep by the sound of the van as it hummed along the highway.

From the midst of a powerful dream I felt Fred gently shaking me awake. "I'm hungry," he said, "And we're only about fifteen miles from a place I really like to eat. Are you hungry?"

I gave him a groggy: "Yeah, thanks for waking me," as I tried to shake the cobwebs in my head from my morning nap. "I just had a dream, a beautiful dream."

"What was the dream?" asked Fred.

I cleared my throat and began.

"I am standing in the middle of a galaxy somewhere in the universe. The accretion disk is circling around my waist. I am a little startled at my size. Also I'm surprised that I am at the middle of this enormous cre-ation. At the same time I am feeling a sense of honor and delight that I have been chosen to be in the position of all that beauty and power. Where I am in the center, there is also a bright light caused by matter exploding into unspeakable power. I am feeling very happy in this pond of planets and stars. I feel thrilled to be alive."

"When I was waking up I thought you were part of the dream."

Fred made a little joke about me being in "la-la-land," but I knew he was intrigued by my dream. I also believe the dream was the catalyst for a real trust between us. It became apparent that he seemed to enjoy talking to me. (Maybe he was reacting to some-thing big and green between my teeth since he got such a huge smile on his face every time I started to talk!) It was obvious he liked my off-the-wall statements like: "If we don't see God in the profane and the profound, we're missing half the picture of our perception of God."

Fred wiggled in his seat to get comfortable, then said with a twist of a smile, "Oh, go ahead Old Man, I'm ready for anything you may have to say. Go ahead, try to shock me!"

I started to ask another question when Fred realized we had been chatting so much that we had missed the turn off for his favorite restaurant. He looked around and saw we needed to pull off the freeway and double back. We didn't mind cause we were having so much fun—missing the turnoff just made us laugh more. We got silly and the conversation progressed from talking about friends to exchanging "potty" jokes like little boys. In a twist so slight, the jokes began to dry up. Fred moved the conversation to a more serious level.

"Old Man," he asked, "What exactly are you doing on the road all alone? You seem to be a bright fellow. What's your story?"

I pursed my lips slightly—he had opened a "can of worms" I thought I wouldn't have to address my first morning on the road. "I'm on a two month sabbatical, living homeless to live more in tune with the people who have to live this way all the time. I grew up poor and had to be very creative in order to have fun. There's a lesson in it for all of us, I think."

Fred wanted to know more, so I continued, "If we're honest with ourselves, then we'll realize each other's sanctity. We're all on the road to the same place. We're just using different means to get there. I don't know if you saw the movie with Steven Segal called *Glimmer Man*? Steven Segal and his sidekick were talking about enlightenment and the different ways people attain it. Steven's way was through meditation and mantra beads which he hung around his neck. He gained strength by praying and centering himself on God and His gifts. Steven's sidekick told him he accomplished the same effect through a bottle of Jack Daniel's whiskey. '

"Deep down we all just want to love one another and love ourselves. Every time I help a stranger, I help myself. It's a real gift to help where help is needed. Sometimes people stop helping because they get burned—or don't see any results. To me the gift is in the doing, not in the results. Whenever we reach out to another person we take the risk of putting ourselves in harm's way. That can be very painful."

Fred looked confused, "What do you mean '...in harm's way?"

"I mean taking a risk doesn't always go smoothly. There are people who take advantage of a loving personality and misinterpret loving as weakness. There are people with evil influences inside of them who will do you harm. But, that mustn't stop us from doing what is right. We've been told from the time we were kids what is dangerous and what is safe. It's up to us to discover for ourselves what that means. Some things that we are warned not to do become kind of like a tape recording inside of us. We have a conditioned response before we can give it a chance to work in our lives. Risk is always part of our lives. We have to decide for ourselves what risks we are willing to take. There are some people who never question boundaries or traditions and some who spend their whole lives questioning everything." I didn't mean to preach although I have to admit it sounded to me as though I was.

There was a brief silence and then Fred said, "I'd say you're one of those who questions."

It didn't take much thought for me to agree with that statement. "I think Gandhi said, 'The truth is the truth, even if you are a minority of one.' People of every era have sought the truth. Just because they have different ways, doesn't mean that they are any farther from the truth than you or I. I guess I am a fan of the Beatitudes; they're the constitution of my faith as a Christian. One of the Beatitudes sticks out in my mind more than any of the rest: 'Blessed are those who are persecuted in the cause of righteousness, for theirs is the kingdom of God.' "

Fred was a character! He got a kick out of me and he seemed to love my way of talking. It seemed he wasn't used to hearing this kind of stuff that was so "out there" and honest.

"Have you ever considered that God is a person?" I asked.

Fred was a little taken aback by the question, but he decided to roll with whatever point I was trying to make. "Pray tell," said Fred. "What do you mean?"

"Oh, you know—God is in everything. That's what I mean. In every child, every rock, every particle of energy."

Fred sniggered a little and said, "Yeah, I was just ribbing you. You and I are just organized differently. My organization of molecules is different from yours. Besides that, I don't believe there is much difference between us in God's eyes."

I exclaimed, "You're right!" I went on, "We are all just organized energy and we are all connected to God, that's for sure. We all have different experiences to share with each other and with God. We're in the process of giving God our life experiences to

"Who is Fred?"

sanctify them. Then God gives us a wonderful gift —LIFE! Life is to play with and to give to our brothers and sisters. I like to think that when I do this I'm giving life back to God in the form of my own personal story. I believe we are each given a road to travel with many twists and turns and forks. It is up to you and me to pick the road that is right for us. When we base our choices on love, then we are on our own personal road to God. Your road is up to you."

"Keep talking, Old Man," Fred encouraged me.

"When we share this gift of love with the people we meet, we can change the world one person at a time." I was quiet for a while, letting this tidbit sink in. Then I said, "When we discover what example we want to give our loved ones, we are called to act on that."

Fred was soaking up each word as I continued, "At this level, there are no students and no teachers. We are each an example to one another. We may have a different perspective that comes from our own personal experiences, but this is the beauty of our calling. That is the beauty of the 'ah-ha!' moment, when we realize we are called to be an example of love. Revelation of the truth is given in our own time, Fred. There is no clock in eternity. We make our personal discovery when God calls us and we say, 'Yes!' to whatever He reveals to us. Of course it takes longer for some of us than for others."

Fred was still quiet. I asked, "Fred, do you believe in coincidences?"

"I'm beginning to wonder about that. What do you think, Old Man?"

"I don't. I believe you and I were meant to meet. I believe that if we missed this opportunity because I had said 'no' to my calling or if you had decided not to pick me up this morning, we would have missed something very important. Even though we would have other opportunities later in our lives, we would have missed a crucial learning time now."

Fred surprised me when he said very seriously, "How can I disagree with what you say when you say it that way? God is all there is. God is the prime mover. He is the power, the truth and the light. He is Love itself!"

I saw Fred's body change in posture and his face brightened. It seemed as though a profound change was coming over him. I felt an overwhelming gratitude that I was privileged to be part of this transforming moment. It was one of those times in my life where I felt the immediate presence of God—much like the birth of my own children

I was delighted to have him express these thoughts, especially since he took a complete 180-degree turn from his original attitude.

"Fred, there are people in our lives who would dispute what we're now agreeing on. We really need all their points of view. We also have to help them through the confusion and the tough spots that we all go through. This helps us as much as it helps them. We all get confused and seek answers—sometimes without even knowing the questions. It is our duty to help others question everything so they can come up with their own God-inspired answers."

We found ourselves excited and agreeing on all of this. We began talking about love and how love doesn't make rational sense and how huge is the idea of love. It seemed every time Fred opened his mouth, I was more impressed by what he was saying and the concepts he was struggling to embrace. Thinking about the enormity of love confused him.

He asked, "If love is really too big to be reasonable, why bother trying to study what it is?" He continued by giving me all his reasons for not exploring love.

I had to stop him to explain again why we need to seek out love in all conditions. "Wherever love is, we need to accept it, as it is, for what it is; or it perverts into something else. It becomes a fear. Fear is the opposite of love. Do you understand the need to continue throughout our lives to find the wisdom in loving?"

Fred knew I was really trying to make a point, but from the look in his eyes, I could see he was having trouble holding on to the concept, let alone the steering wheel.

I tried to re-phrase: "I am talking about unconditional acceptance of a person where they are in their life, right now—no strings attached. That is the unconditional love that God has for each of us. God accepts us right now as we are—not as He would like us to be, but as we are."

The reality of the idea of unconditional love was brand new to Fred. He phased in and out of understanding and enthusiasm. He stated he now had a new "happiest moment" in his life—his experience of feeling the love of God flowing freely through him and the feeling of freedom it brought.

Four and a half hours of driving had given Fred a lifetime of experiences to revise. When we finally reached the quaint little diner, we were still talking about love.

We got out of the van and as we entered the diner Fred said, "You know, Old Man, you lost me when you were talking about everyone being one in the spirit, but somehow I now understand."

The diner looked like a small house on the side of the freeway. The parking lot was filled with trucks—a sure sign that the food ought to be good. We entered by the front door and the waitress came to escort us to an empty table in the rear of the room that could hold only ten tables.

"You're gonna love Edna's chili and meat loaf sandwiches," Fred assured me. "Just let me do the ordering, it's on me."

When the waitress, May, came to our table, Fred introduced me to her as Old Man. She took his order and went back to the kitchen.

Fred appeared to love the diner and commented, "Yeah, this place is always jumping. Usually there is a guy washing dishes in back who helps with the cooking and ordering, but I don't see him."

Fred went on to tell me how he had discovered this place the first time he tried to leave home. He called it his "little bit of heaven."

As May brought the food to our table, I could see a stack of dishes in the kitchen. Keeping in mind Fred's comment about the dishwasher and seeing the two ladies were swamped; I asked May if they could use some help with the dishes.

"Have you ever used a steamer before?" she asked.

"Yes, I have. If you would like, I would be happy to help you catch up until the crowd dies down a little."

May told me that she couldn't pay much, but if I would be willing to put on an apron and get started; she'd make sure I got a little something. In fact, I was willing to work for free just to prove to them that I was a good worker.

Fred and I finished our food, which was excellent. He could see I was going to stay to work in the kitchen. Without much further comment he got up and left the diner. I figured he was gone and I'd never see him again. He'd left an impression on me—I just hoped I'd had some effect on him.

A feeling of peace came over me as I donned an apron and approached the steamer. I began to sing to myself. Retrieving the first tray of dishes, I busied myself with the task at hand. The work was hot and hard and fast moving. I felt very satisfied.

May came back into the kitchen area and I saw a huge smile brighten her face. She watched as I quickly dispatched pile after pile of dirty dishes.

Old Man's work with May and Edna

Just as I was about to steam the second set of dishes, I could see Fred coming through the doorway into the diner. He came back to the kitchen where I was.

"You know, I really didn't want to leave before thanking you for what you did," he said. "You see there's been a lot of confusion in my life, especially in the last few months. You have helped me see that maybe my folks really do love me. I guess God put us together today for a reason. I'm gonna go home."

On the way out Fred stopped at the counter and thanked May for giving Old Man a job for the day. I watched out the window as his van pulled away. I was grateful he had returned to tell me his plan, but I was also sad I would never see him again. He'd become a friend in a few short hours. I was really happy he'd decided to go home. At that moment I had an overwhelming feeling of the presence of God. Tears of joy welled up in my eyes as I watched Fred drive off. He'd reminded me of the mystical way love moves in our lives. I was to think of Fred often as I ambled my way across this vast beautiful country over the next several weeks. He was the first in a long line of wonderful people I met who taught me so many life lessons.

CHAPTER 3

The diner was small—ten tables and a counter that sat four. The place was always packed—not just because the food was so good, but also because there was a truck brake inspection station next door. The women were so busy waiting on customers that they let the dishes pile up not only in the kitchen, but on the tables as well.

I had been working only a short time. The kitchen was wall-to-wall slop and grunge, but after a few loads of dishes completed, I turned my attention to the front. I began to clear tables and sweep the floor; making the dining area way more presentable. Then I returned to the kitchen wondering how, in the name of God, anyone could find room to cook in such squalor. The hours flew by with a steady flow of customers until the doors were closed at 10:00 p.m. I was exhausted. I asked May when their dishwasher was returning.

"His little boy is sick and he had to take him to the doctor. He'll call us in the morning and let us know what is happening," she answered. "In the meantime, do you want to stay until he comes back?"

I was thrilled at the prospect of work on my first day out and quickly answered, "Yes!"

Although the "Closed" sign was out, there were still a few people in the room sitting over late night coffee. At this little oasis on
the road, everyone seemed to know each other. I asked what town
we were in and was told we weren't in a town—"just a truck stop
in the woods."

When the last customer had left, May locked the door. That
was the first opportunity I had to introduce myself to Edna, the
cook. She commented, "I like the way you work. You're quiet, you
get the job done. Keep it up and we'll see you bright and early at
6:00 a.m.!"

I helped the women clean up the place. It was after midnight
when I heard, "Phew" simultaneously from both women signal-
ing the end of a very busy, difficult day. The kitchen was spotless
to begin the next day that was a mere six hours away. May and
Edna bid me goodnight and went off to the adjoining house.

After the long day I'd had I was ready for sleep. With May's
permission, I planned to roll out my sleeping bag among some
trees in back of the restaurant near the truck stop. She had warned
me that the noise might keep me awake, but I was so tired I knew
I could sleep through the rumbling and clanging of the all-night
trucker traffic.

I made a cushion of pine needles where I placed my sheet of
plastic and topped it with my sleeping bag. This was my first night
on the road. I lay down, fully clothed with all my worldly possessions by my side in the backpack. I listened for a while to the
sounds of the trucks. Soon the hum of the engines wasn't even
noticed. I reveled in the stars I glimpsed through the branches of
the tree that was my shelter. All manner of sounds and thoughts
swirled in my head as I drifted off into my first night's sleep.

I awakened in a field of diamonds; just as a piece of sun burst
it's way through a deep blanket of tulle fog. The meadow was
moist with tiny dewdrops glistening from each pine needle. "Ah,"

I thought, "So this was to be my pay each day, Lord. A gift even before I arise from my bed."

The singing of the birds was muted by fog and the furious fluttering of winged insects and the clatter of engines roaring into life. Over the rumble, I heard one trucker shout, "Hey, Bill, what time is it?"

When Bill responded, "It's 5:20, I knew I would have no need for an alarm clock to wake me in the mornings.

Looking around at my gear, I began my first attempt at a morning ritual. With as little as I had, I did not suspect how time consuming this could be. This first morning was a particular adventure. Somewhere in the night, I had inexplicably lost a sock and the Cliff Bar I had intended for my breakfast. I searched for about ten minutes, trying to understand how they could have disappeared. When I paused to scratch my head in confusion, I heard a sound come through the morning fog. The sound seemed fairly close—a rustle of plastic and the distinct sound of chewing. Finding the source I got the giggles. Barely visible through the fog, about 100 feet away, I spied a baby raccoon, resting comfortably on my sock and peeling the wrapper of *my* Cliff Bar! By the time I got to him my Cliff Bar was almost gone, but I wanted my sock!

"Shoo, you little varmint!" I ordered.

This startled him enough to move away. Unfortunately, his right rear paw had become entangled in my sock. As he walked away, he was indeed a comical sight, alternately walking and hopping and shaking his foot to get rid of the sock!

I followed him into the bushes, where his mother and two siblings were enjoying their raid on my camp—they had more of my Cliff Bars. I got a good laugh, but they got my sock. When I ordered, "Get out of here you little thieves!" they readily obeyed.

The four of them waddled off into the fog, the little one dancing along wearing my sock. "Oh well," I thought, "I guess I didn't need that sock anyway."

The little thief

Dressing in the white shirt and black pants I had brought (just in case I got work), I appeared in the diner with my backpack. I knew better than to leave my possessions outside—they just weren't safe outside!

I was feeling pretty smug about the way I had gotten a job on the first day. I was sure it was God's plan that I have this job (even though it was May and Edna who hired me because of my good work).

May was wiping down a plastic tablecloth. When I entered she surprised me by simply asking: "Can you come back a little later today, say about four o'clock?"

"Sure I can," I answered. I knew the dishes would be piled high by then. "Okay, then, see you at four." I backed out of the door and wondered where God wanted me to go that day.

Choosing from among my directional signs, I placed "North" on my backpack. I figured Portland was only a few hours away. I thought I could easily make it there and back by four o'clock.

God was smiling on my travel plans. Within a few minutes I was in a car going straight to Portland. The couple that picked me up was deep into their own conversation. I had a quiet ride. Eventually, as we neared the city, I commented to them that they could drop me anywhere. Without any acknowledgement that they had even heard me they stopped on the highway off-ramp and indicated I could get out. I thanked them for the ride, but they drove off without any acknowledgment. I stood there alone on the Sunset Highway and just thanked God for the ride and the couple who had provided it.

With a deep breath I felt the cool air of the morning fill my lungs. I felt free as a bird. I commented to myself, "Where am I? I wonder where the homeless people hang out in this city." (The more time I spent alone over the next weeks, the more I had these conversations with myself.) Today, I was really glad there was no one around to hear me.

I looked across the street and toward a large building that I discovered was Saint Vincent's Hospital. It was a beautiful sight and a great morning for a stroll. Laden with my backpack, I sauntered under an overpass toward the hospital. I encountered several Latino men standing on the street. It seemed they were waiting to be picked up for a day's work (much like the Mexican men wait around my home town).

In my very broken Spanish, I asked one man where I could find a park or maybe a visitor's center for the hospital.

"You should stick to English, my friend," the man told me in pretty clear English.

"Sorry," I answered.

Then he politely answered my question with a point of his finger. I stopped at a nearby phone and checked in with May and Edna. It was just a little after 8:00 a.m.

May answered the phone and thanked me for calling. She said, "The dishwasher's son is sicker than he thought. It looks like you can have a job here as long as you can stay."

I was flattered that they liked my work, but I didn't want to become too settled. I replied, "Thanks, May, I can probably stay as long as a week. I really need to head East after that. Will that be okay?"

May was happy enough to know that I could stay at least a week. She offered me a dollar more an hour. (They had paid me $35.00 for the work of the day before.) I was pleased with the money—especially since I had asked for nothing.

There was a lot of traffic on the streets of Portland, but the homeless population was rather invisible. I wondered where they would be at this time of the morning. As noon approached, I quickened my pace looking for them. No matter where I went the homeless eluded my search. I had to leave the city feeling a sense of urgency at having missed the opportunity to hang out with the street people—wherever they were.

I managed a slow walk back to Highway 5 where I was going to grab a ride south to the diner. Once again, providence smiled on me. With barely a moment's wait, a young couple came along in their car. They were on their way to Idaho with their family and gave me a ride to the door of the diner. I was tempted to continue east with them, but I knew it was more important to keep my commitment to May and Edna. I thanked them for the ride and headed into the diner.

"Hi, May," I said.

"Hi," She answered. "You're not supposed to be here 'til four —and it's only 2:30. It's good you're here early, we can really use your help."

I hoped I could charm some food out of them before I started working. The lone Cliff Bar I had salvaged earlier in the morning was all I had eaten. When May asked if I'd like to start work right after having something to eat, I was overjoyed! However, it was not to be. May was going past me with a tray loaded with plates of food and I watched in slow motion as she missed the table and the tray and food landed in the lap of her customer. Without missing a beat, I set down my backpack and ran to the back of the restaurant to retrieve a dustpan and a broom.

"Oh, my gosh, I'm so sorry!" May repeated over and over.

As I arrived with the clean-up tools, the man broke the tension when he good-naturedly asked, "Ya got some bread to sop up this soup in my lap?"

From that instant I was drawn into service. When Edna finally asked if I was hungry, it was already 4:30 p.m. By then I was on a roll and couldn't stop to eat. Besides, I rationalized; they probably hadn't eaten either.

The customers loved them. May and Edna were great company because they would laugh and chat about anything that came into their minds. These were two "salt-of-the-earth" women whose values represented the best of the American dream.

"How did you meet Fred?" they asked when we had a short break.

In the flurry of work, I had forgotten they knew Fred. I answered, "I was hitchhiking out of Ashland and he gave me a ride. We had never met before that. I wish I could have really said good-bye to him."

"That's okay, honey," they said. "He'll come through here again and we'll tell him for you."

They both went on talking with everyone who came in. As I cleared the tables and washed the dishes they greeted each customer as if he or she were a long-lost friend. The steamer was so hot; I couldn't tell whether my skin was soaked with dishwater or sweat. My black pants and white shirt were so drenched that as I cleared one table the customer asked me if there was a swimming pool out back!

As the day passed into evening the business never slowed. From my place at the steamer, I couldn't see if it was light or dark outside. The hours melted into one another. On one trip to the front I noticed a long line of customers waiting for tables. Edna was such a good cook and her work was so endless, I feared she would have a heart attack—she was no spring chicken. I wondered how these two sweet ladies kept up from day to day. I was very glad I could lighten their load even for a short time.

Ten o'clock closing arrived mercifully for all of us. It was rather like the closing bell on the stock market. Once the door was locked, Edna and May dropped into chairs and collapsed from a job well done. We were all exhausted, but happy to be in each other's company.

"How long have you two been doing this?" I asked.

May replied, "We've been cooking and cleaning all our lives. Sometimes fourteen hours a day. We left Missouri together in '52. We had decided to combine our savings and open a diner. We was both good cooks. We been doin' it ever since. But I do feel like we slowin' down."

"Now, we told you what we done. What makes you tick? And why do you call yourself 'Old Man'?" chimed in Edna.

I was just getting the last piece of Edna's pecan pie and took a bite to give myself some time as I tried to think of what I wanted to tell them. There was a long silence as they waited. All I could say was "This is really good pie."

The two women looked at each other and asked if I was running from the law, "seeing as how you want all your pay in cash."

I told them the basics of my story: "This kind of work has always kept me close to the Lord. I figure that if I can do what makes me happy and do the Lord's work at the same time, then the rest of my life is pretty much window dressing. Prayer has always been a major part of my life and this work helps me concentrate in that."

May and Edna's joint

May seemed a million miles away. I offered: "A penny for your thoughts, May."

"You made me think what life is like away from this damn diner. Ya know, Edna," said May, "We haven't taken a vacation from this place in five years."

Edna laughed and said: "I thought something else was on your mind the way you was wiping the soup off that guy this afternoon."

We all had a good laugh when May replied, "What about life away from this damn diner? What about you and me going to Tahiti or somewhere like that for a year or so?"

That brought another laugh, but there was something more serious in her tone as she said: "Edna, let's go to Las Vegas for a few days. What about it? What if we could go out every night and gamble some. What d'ya say?"

Edna was getting interested and now also had a more serious look on her face. "And how'd you propose we pay for this vacation? Who'd take over the diner?"

I'm sure she was thinking about the balance in their bank account. They both looked to me for advice. "What d'ya think Old Man?"

"I'm honored you'd include me in your decision making, but I'm different than either of you."

This brought a long dual stare in my direction. They kept their eyes on me until I blurted: "I'd go for it! Fly away! Have fun!"

In spite of the late hour, a new spark had come into the eyes of the two women. They began to talk about the possibilities. They had become kind of excited about the idea of a vacation! They were like a couple of schoolgirls having fun!

I picked up my backpack and told them I'd be back at work early in the morning if they thought they still needed me. I walked them to the door of their little attached bungalow. May invited, "You're welcome to sleep on the couch in the living room."

"No, thanks," I said. "I'm just getting used to being outside. I really don't mind the sound of the trucks starting their engines next to my ear." Though I thought to myself that the odor of diesel fuel did interfere with that fresh morning smell that I usually found so agreeable.

"Be here at 5:30," Edna said, Tomorrow is a big day."

In the middle of the night—probably around 3:00 a.m.—a light rain began to fall. The tree that sheltered me deflected most of the moisture. I was dry and cozy and glad I had remembered my brother's childhood camping advice about sleeping under trees.

Five o'clock arrived and my inner alarm woke me up from a very sound sleep. The sun was just lighting the low-lying fog creating a beautiful wake-up glow. I broke camp and stowed my gear much easier this second morning out. Thank God there were no raccoons this morning! I headed off for the diner and in my sleepy stupor thanked God for the friends I had met and the job I had.

When I walked into the diner, May and Edna were already working. Their ongoing dialogue this morning was about their possible vacation. I covered my now dirty clothes with a clean apron and greeted them.

May stopped her scrubbing, turned to me and said: " Edna and I have been talking about giving you ten percent of our tips and a little more hourly wage."

"I'm really happy you want to be so generous with me. This will be until your regular dishwasher comes back, right?" I replied.

"Yeah," said Edna, "and maybe we could keep you a little longer, too."

I just let the subject drop. I really didn't want to stay here too long. I had places to go and new challenges to meet.

The day flowed like we had worked together for years. The hours were long and hot, but the women's company was so pleasant that the time flew. As we came to the end of day two, the smells from the open campfires around the rest stop assailed me. I loved sleeping outside.

The third morning I sprinted into the diner at 5:30 a.m. for my coffee. May greeted me with the cash payment for my first two days of work. At this point, I felt I needed to remind her that I was a temporary worker. I was a little worried that they might just think I 'd changed my mind because we were having so much fun. But my reminder wasn't acknowledged because they were already focused on the work for the day.

May said, "It looks like we're not gonna need you this morning, so you can do whatever you like til about 2:00 o'clock. When you come back I have a friend I want you to meet. His name is Jack. You'll like him."

I was a little confused, but asked them if I could leave my backpack behind the counter. I headed out with a crisp $20.00 bill in my hand and the rest of my wages in my sock. With a song in my heart, kicking a rock ahead of me, I began my walk toward Highway 5.

This time I used my thumb to get an almost immediate ride. The man behind the wheel asked the usual questions and then listened to the radio for the rest of the journey into Portland. I wanted to return to the same part of town where I'd been the previous day, so I asked him to let me off at the Sunset Highway overpass.

Thanking him for the ride, I walked past the hospital into a park where I saw a man, woman, and little girl huddled together. As I approached, the child cowered behind the woman. I could see the man was tall. He appeared to be in his early thirties, wearing a dark brown coat the pockets bulging from the contents. The woman in her late twenties had dirty blond hair and was wearing a dark blue coat. The child was about three feet tall with long straight dark hair held in place with barrettes.

I'd had lots of experience with people on the street and it seemed to me this was a family in crisis.

Approaching them I said, "Hi," as gently as possible. "Are you hungry?"

Without speaking, the man looked up at me and nodded.

"I'm going across the street to get some food, I'll get you something to eat and drink." I knelt down in front of the little girl saying, "Do you want a coke or a milkshake?"

"A milkshake, please."

I asked, "Do you like chocolate, vanilla or strawberry?"

The man answered for her: "She likes strawberry."

Within a few minutes I was back. As I passed food items to them, the woman broke down. Tears flowed down her cheeks. It was clear they were desperate.

The man interjected, "Thanks, mister, I don't have money or…"

I stopped him and said: "Just do the same for someone else when you see the need."

I knew it might be quite a while before this would happen, but I wanted to plant the seed for him to be open to helping someone else who might have a similar need in the future. I also hoped I could give them some hope that their circumstances would change.

The newly homeless and scared to death.

I ate with them on the grass in front of the hospital and asked where they lived. (They looked to me as if they were homeless.)

"My wife and I both worked for UPS until two weeks ago, then there was a strike and they laid off everyone around here. We didn't have enough money to pay the rent or the bills. We had to take Ginny out of school and we've been sleeping out here the last three days. It's scary."

Because of my experience in California, I knew there was help available—we just had to look. When people are newly homeless they often have no idea where to turn. There is a big knowledge gap when it comes to public service agencies. After a few phone calls, with full stomachs, I had located a family shelter that would take them in. We hailed a cab and the mother told Ginny to give me a hug. Both parents thanked me and climbed into the safety of the cab for the journey to the shelter.

Thanking God for this latest opportunity, I headed back to the freeway to find my own ride "home." I was back at the diner before two. I changed into my work clothes and apron once again ready to tackle the dishes. May was talking with one of the customers I recognized as a regular patron. She summoned me and introduced me to Jack.

"Hello," he said. "May tells me you can drive a bobtail and that you have a Class II license. Is that true?"

Wondering where he was going with this information, I answered: "Yes, that is true."

Apparently Jack and May had been talking for some time before I arrived. Now May excused herself saying: "I'm glad you're back right on time, looks like you and Jack have some talking to do."

Once she was gone, Jack began: "May tells me that the dishwasher's son is getting better and he is coming back to work tomorrow."

This was the first time I'd been privy to this news. In fact, just then the dishwasher, himself, appeared and came over to meet me. He was pretty scruff with long sideburns and dirty fingernails. He thanked me for helping out while he was gone and said he'd be back pretty soon.

Jack and I talked for quite some time. We both agreed to meet the next day for a test of my driving skills. Jack needed a driver to take a truck east.

Again that day the diner was busy and the time passed quickly as the customers came and went. I was so grateful for the past days —my encounter with Fred and meeting May and Edna. I was excited about the possibilities of driving for Jack. What else did God have in store for me?

After the close of the restaurant and about an hour or so of good conversation with May and Edna, I picked up my backpack and headed for my tree at about 11:00 p.m. I was too excited about the prospect of getting a job as a driver to sleep much that night. I was up early the next morning remembering Psalm 23 and praying: "The Lord is my shepherd, there is nothing I shall want."

I was ready! Maybe I hadn't had much sleep, but I felt completely refreshed, ready to do whatever God put in front of me. With my first cup of coffee in hand, I exclaimed to anyone who could hear: "Life is good!"

By 6:00 a.m. I met Jack at the door of the diner. He was standing in front of a 24-foot moving van with a compartment over the cab.

"That's a nice truck," I said, circling it and inspecting it for damage. By now I knew he was going to ask me to drive this truck somewhere if I passed the driving test.

Jack lifted his right hand to his shirt pocket and removed a set of keys. He threw them to me saying in his rough morning voice, "You're the driver!"

I continued to walk around the rig, inspecting the tires and shocks. Satisfied with my inspection, I climbed into the cab. Feeling like a kid in a candy store, I noticed a five-speed transmission and I knew I was going to have some fun! I turned the key in the ignition and the truck started immediately. I did a final check of the brake lights, running lights and turn signals and pronounced all satisfactory.

"Well, where do you want to go?" I asked.

"Turn right out of the parking lot and follow the road for about a quarter of a mile."

After a couple of turns and bends we came to the gate of an old junkyard. We passed a man standing in the guard shack. Jack asked me to stop. Getting out of the truck, he said, "Now I want you to drive through the yard and come back here. Can you handle that?"

"Sure," I said; in spite of the fact that I saw one main road heading in with several roads branching off in different directions.

When I had made a few wrong turns and hit several dead ends where I had to do some pretty fancy turning around, I finally made it back to the guard shack. Jack looked very pleased that I had not taken out the side of the truck and the attendant in the shack called out, "Looks like you got a live one this time, Jack!"

Jack got back into the cab of the truck and directed me out the dirt road away from the junkyard. Asking me to pull over and stop, he got behind the wheel.

"Do you need a ride anywhere?" he asked.

"Well, I'd like to go into Portland for a few hours before I work my last shift at the diner. It looks like I'm out of a job now that the dishwasher's back."

Jack had little to say on the ride into Portland. What he did say was enough to seal the direction for the rest of my trip: "Ya know Old Man, or whatever your real name is (he had not asked to see my license); May is a real nice lady, but sometimes she lines me up with some real losers. That's why I may have seemed a little hard at first. Ya see I had to know what I was dealing with."

I told him that was perfectly understandable. "You must get pretty tired of road-testing guys who don't know a standard transmission from an automatic."

"Yeah, it's pitiful," said Jack. "Would you be interested in taking a driving job when you get things settled at the diner?"

"Where would I be going?"

"Denver," said Jack with a little smirk. "Won't be able to pay much. Just like May, I'll be paying cash—under the table. If you do a good job getting the truck to my cousin in Denver, he might want you to continue on with a full van to Mobile, Alabama—but only if you get the truck to him in one piece."

I could hardly believe my ears. This was a dream come true. "So, what you're saying is that the truck you give me will be empty. You just want me to drive it to Denver, right?"

"Yeah, you want the job?"

I replied, "I'll meet you at the diner tomorrow morning at six, okay?"

"That's perfect," Jack agreed as he let me out in Portland.

Later that day I was back in the kitchen one last time. As I put on my apron, I was thinking about the family in Portland. I had not seen them that morning, but in my imagination I could see the little girl, Ginny, on the playground after she'd had her lunch the previous day. I hoped they would be all right. I faced the dilemma of why I was there—was it to help them and others like them or to work? Finally the light dawned on me and I realized that I wouldn't have been able to help them if I didn't have the wages from Edna and May. Besides, Denver was looking very sweet.

My thoughts shifted to May and Edna. I had grown fond of them and I know they liked me too. Less than a week ago, I had to stop and think about each step in the sanitizing of these dishes, now I had the satisfaction of a job relearned and a job well done. I liked waking early in the morning and feeling the first beads of sweat roll down my face as I loaded the steamer. I liked the repetitiveness of doing the same thing over and over. It was a simple and good life experience, very reminiscent of my youth when I worked at the café in my hometown.

As I worked on through that last day in the diner, I found myself feeling a tremendous gratitude. I quietly sang one of my favorite songs: *"If you want to live life free, take your time, go slowly. Do few things, but do them well, simple things are holy. Day by day, stone by stone; build your secret slowly. Day by day, you'll grow too. You'll know heaven's glory."* I'd interrupt each line with my heartfelt mantra, "Life is good!"

The entire day I hummed and praised God for this happy time in my life. I felt a brief sadness as I closed the steamer for the last time. Then it was time to go. I walked over to May who was focused on scrubbing an already clean table. I wrapped my arms around her, giving her a hug in thanksgiving for all the happiness she'd shared and the opportunities that she'd opened for me. "I pray that I run into many such as you wherever I go May."

She tried to be upbeat about the situation by relying on her usual humor. "Now don't you go expecting me or Edna to get up to see you off. We need our beauty sleep, you know."

I suggested to them both that they declare a holiday for themselves and let the dishwasher take over. I reminded them to think about the vacation we'd been talking about. "You really deserve it! So do it!" I said.

I turned to them as I walked out the door. "I'm going to miss you both—a lot!"

What a way to begin my time being homeless. It was obvious to me that I was not guiding this journey. The hellos and good-byes were ebbing and flowing in my life like a river—the river of life.

For the last time, I went back to my spot in the woods. I stretched out under my favorite tree and peacefully fell asleep.

Dawn broke and my morning prayer was one of gratitude for another beautiful day—not to be taken for granted—another day to be thankful for every breath of life, every beat of my heart. My mood was a mixture of joy and bliss—pure gift. I had everything to look forward to and nothing to regret. Slipping out of my sleeping bag, it was zip-snap-zap and I was ready to take off. It was 5:45 a.m. and I wanted to beat Jack to the diner.

CHAPTER 4

Listening to the symphony of diesel trucks pulling in and out, I waited for Jack. As he pulled into the parking area and got out of the truck, I greeted him with an energetic and happy, "Good morning!"

He made no attempt to respond. I figured he wasn't a morning person. He fumbled around in his shirt pocket and pulled out an envelope. "Use the cash for gas, lodging and food. Good luck." Then the man of few words continued, "Oh, yeah, I'm gonna need a ride around the corner, back to the yard."

At the yard, he took me into the office to give me a map and a phone number to use when I arrived in Denver. He bristled when I said I had a question. "What!" he barked.

"Does your cousin in Denver expect I'll be coming back to Denver or did you tell him I wanted this to be a one-way ride?"

"He knows all about your wantin' to keep goin' east. Neither him nor me have any plans of you comin' back this way. Okay? It doesn't matter. Anyway, his foreman in Mobile, Curtis, prob'ly won't like you. He's pretty conservative."

I thanked him for his candor and took the map. My head was still reeling at the great fortune of being able to get all the way to Mobile, Alabama. On my walk back to the truck Jack reminded me what a risk he was taking by letting me drive. He wanted to make darn sure I understood his situation. "I really don't know what my cousin, Maury, has in store for you when you reach Denver, but I wish you the best of luck."

The truck loomed ahead of me like a giant orange Tonka truck. The door handle was above my head—so I had to jump up to get settled in. I turned to thank Jack, put the key in the ignition, depressed the clutch, put the truck in gear and headed for the interstate.

About fifteen miles down the road I stopped at a convenience store to buy two large coffees and make a quick inspection of the map Jack had given me. I had only one expectation of this road trip—that it be joyful. I knew there could be flat tires or other mishaps in the middle of nowhere. But I also knew I could dictate my response to them. Gosh, darn it! I was going to have fun!

I drove through some of the most beautiful country I had ever seen—surely the most beautiful places in North America. Driving along Highway 84, the Columbia River winding along beside me, I couldn't stop singing. I was so happy. I prayed in thanksgiving for this time and made a personal invitation to Jesus to sit beside me along the way to get a good look at what God, our father had created for us. On that day, on that road, on the way to my first stop in Boise, Idaho the past met the present moment in a triumphant embrace. Emotions gripped me and reality broke over me in alternating waves of déjà vu, joy and chaos. It was the perfect storm of emotions!

I remembered my younger years as a musician when travel was a daily exhausting and lonely adventure. Over and over this day I repeated to myself, "I am so happy that I am living a life where I'm allowed to follow my dream."

I knew that dreams come with no guarantee of being fulfilled. I was intent on trying to fulfill these dreams.

CHAPTER 5

Driving along, enjoying the country-
side, I surprisingly found myself caught up in the beginnings of a
wave of loneliness. Thoughts of my family intruded into my
enjoyment. I already missed them. But these thoughts of family
also helped me balance the perspective of my calling to be homeless. This would be a temporary calling.

It was mid-afternoon and time to stop for that second cup of
coffee—now long cold. While I was resting my feet on the dash-
board listening to the radio, I watched the ballet of traffic moving
through the scenery around me. Brahms' second symphony
played and a hawk circled the river's edge in search of a meal. The
hawk floated lazily for a while on the invisible current, buffeted
by the waves of air as I was bombarded by the waves of my
thoughts. Recognizing there would be hard times ahead, I told
myself out loud, "That will be then and this is now. Be content
with this moment."

Many songs churned in my mind as I turned the key and got
back into motion. In a burst of cosmic energy one of my favorite
songs (one I had performed hundreds of times on stage) came on
the radio. I bounced up and down along the road singing: "*A
month of nights, a year of days, October's drifting into Mays. You set*

your sails when the tide comes in and you just cast your fate to the wind." This was a happy magical moment. The sad loneliness dissipated, I reveled in the joy that comes from doing exactly what I knew I was supposed to be doing at this very moment.

Reveling in the now I found my mind being drawn to past memories. My family of birth consisted of Mother and Father and two brothers, Gaylord and Darrell. My Father died when I was two and Mother had a hard time keeping us together. She worked full time and had a series of women who took care of us. Some of these women were pretty cruel.

Mother became a regular customer at the local bar. She would drag Gaylord and me with her and we would play under the pool table. The owner finally asked Mother not to bring us with her because we caused too much commotion. Mother met her second husband, Jack, at the bar.

Jack was a good man who loved Mother and cared for her three sons like we were his own. Thoughts of Jack accepting three growing boys caused me to reflect on how difficult that must have been. Before he met Mother, he was alone.

Once Mother married Jack, our lives changed a lot. We ate regularly and had clean clothes. With two incomes many aspects of our lives were easier.

My real father's mother was still a huge part of our lives. Grandma Franklin was a force to be reckoned with. She took over my spiritual well being, making sure I attended Sunday services with her at the Baptist Church. Of course that was after Saturday nights that I spent in the company of her second husband; not my real Grandpa, but the one I called Grandpa.

Grandpa and I would watch Big-Time Wrestling together on the television. Grandpa loved wrestling, I loved the four scoops of velvety vanilla ice cream drenched in homemade strawberry preserves! My recollection is that most of the ice cream landed in my mouth, but I may be wrong about that because Grandma always put me in the bath after I ate the ice cream. She ruled with an iron hand!

Sunday mornings started with Sunday school and then an hour and a half in church listening to a "Hell and damnation" sermon by the Reverend. I didn't mind the preaching because the minister was a wonderful man who packed great charisma into his denunciation of the evils of the world.

One particularly bright Sunday morning I saw a new face in the class. Johnny was a boy just my age (11 at the time). I learned his family had moved to our town, Pomona, from someplace in the mid west. Johnny and I became the best of friends and each week we could hardly wait to sit next to each other during the long sermons. One of those mornings, the pastor told the congregation that Charlie, one of our church elders, was going to lead a weekend revival for the young people in the mountains of Big Bear. Johnny and I were really excited at the prospect of spending two whole days together and we both signed up right after the service was finished. We were given forms to take home for our parents to sign.

I ran into the house, excited to show Mother my form and to tell her about this weekend when I'd get to go to the mountains with Johnny. Mother's only comment was, "No!"

I learned she didn't have the $10.00 fee that was required. I was heartbroken. But when my devastating news reached Charlie, he somehow made it possible for me to go.

Friday afternoon finally arrived and I met Johnny in the church parking lot with my bedroll. We were loaded into the bus along with our belongings. Johnny and I sat together as we drove the sixty miles to the camp in the mountains. I still remember the windy road leading to the crunchy gravel drive into the campground. We reached our destination where the driveway circled around a grass area outlined with white painted rocks. In the middle of the circle of grass stood a flagpole with the flag flapping merrily in the breeze. An L-shaped building beckoned. It was the most beautiful sight I had ever seen.

We scrambled out of the bus. I looked up the hill at a skyline of trees. Around me were well-worn paths going in every direction. We were led into the main hall, with it's huge fireplace and double sliding glass doors. It was almost evening by the time we had checked out our bunk areas. Soon we were called to prayer before dinner and then we shared a great meal cooked by Sherri, the wife of Gary who was in charge of the camp.

Gary, an educated man, was the assistant pastor of our church. He may have been in charge, but it was Charlie who was the real draw. Charlie was a very spiritual man. He'd been a boxer early in his life, but now he seemed to be about 75 years old. He had a face all the kids loved. He also had a way of scooping up sad children in his big arms. We all loved Charlie.

After dinner we had evening stories. Gary told us stories about the Bible. Charlie told us true-life stories about his life as a former sinner. They both talked about how the Lord saved their souls and how the Lord wanted us to be saved.

Johnny and I were just happy to be there together. Charlie made sure we were in the same group during the day on Saturday. We played games and listened to more talks. The day was filled with fun activities and great meals. Just before dinner, we had free time to walk with someone on staff or with a friend. The only rule was to stay within sight of the compound.

Johnny and I walked together. We agreed that we liked this "revival." We thought it was lots better than school. We liked this place so much we never wanted to leave. I suppose, in our own way, we had dedicated ourselves to the Lord.

After walking for most of the free time, we sat down to watch a volleyball game that was going on near the cafeteria. Suddenly I wanted to be alone. I got up and asked Johnny if he minded if I walked by myself for a while. He said, "O.K."

I could see the sun beginning to go down behind an A-frame chapel that stood on the top of the hill. It was a beautiful sight and I *stopped to take in this beauty. I felt really happy. I felt like the Lord must be here. I felt a strong desire to go up into the chapel to sit. The sun glimmered through the windows of the chapel drawing me up the hill. I was feeling so good as I opened the door.*

It was semi-dark inside the chapel. The outlines of people's heads came into focus as I heard a collective gasp. The heads turned one by one and through the dim light I could see the eyes of the counselors looking at me. The lights went on and several women burst into tears while other people's eyes met mine. I saw a vacant aisle seat and immediately sat down, trying to be invisible. People around me were exclaiming, "Praise Jesus!" as they began to exit the small building. Some patted me on the shoulder as they went by. Others were mumbling prayers of gratitude. Completely dumbfounded, I sat until Charlie came over to me with tears in his eyes. Grabbing me in his great bear hug he exclaimed, "Son, you're the one!" Then he walked out of the chapel, following the rest of the counselors.

His words went through me with a great surge of power. I sat alone in the chapel reflecting in my eleven-year-old mind on what had just happened. I had no idea what it all meant. But it felt good. When the dinner bell rang I left the chapel and walked slowly down the hill. No one ever mentioned this event to me again. And I was too young and naïve to think about approaching them.

Caught up in my reverie, I came back to earth in the truck speeding down the road east. I don't know what Charlie meant all those years ago. But here I was today on my own journey and it was heading into night. I was getting tired from my long day's drive and it was time to rest. I looked for a wide spot in the road. I needed just a few hours of sleep. I spotted a gravel area just ahead, pulled over out of the way of traffic and settled into a most comfortable sleeping position in the cab of the truck. It felt so good to close my tired eyes.

Suddenly I was startled awake by the flashing lights of a police car. Quickly, I sat up and rolled down my window as the officer approached. I greeted him with "Hello officer, have I done something wrong?"

He went through the drill of license, registration, proof of insurance and phoned to make sure the truck wasn't stolen. Returning my license, he said, "You can't sleep here."

I drove off to look for a designated rest stop, while he made a u-turn across double yellow lines.

I was well past Cheyenne, Wyoming, and at least two hours past safe driving time when I finally found a rest area. Pulling over, I turned off the motor, stretched out on the seat and shut my eyes, immediately falling into a deep sleep.

Four hours later I resumed consciousness and walked into the rest room to wash my face so I could begin day two in the truck. The water felt so good on my face I decided to continue cleansing my upper torso. I was dripping under my arms when I realized there were no more paper towels and I would have to resort to the blow dryer. With my shirt off, I had both arms in the air, when a little boy walked in and asked if I was being held up! He left in such a hurry that I had no time to respond. I guess I did look pretty strange!

I felt very rested as I got back onto the freeway heading toward Denver. I was surprised at how good I could feel on so little sleep. I prayed as I drove and had a feeling of real peace. The more peaceful I felt, the more I prayed. The more I prayed, the more at peace I felt.

In a spirit of goodwill, I stopped for a young couple thumbing a ride. They ran to the truck and thanked me for stopping. It was apparent they were stoned, but I invited them to put their gear in the back of the truck. They complained loudly about waiting over an hour to get picked up. They also insisted that they could keep their belongings on their laps inside the cab. I thought they must have had some bad experience of being robbed and needed to have their possessions within reach.

Without asking, they each pulled out a pack of cigarettes and each helped the other light up. The smell of weed filled the truck cab. I told them I had an allergy to smoke—would they mind putting out the cigarettes. The young man said, "Chill out, man. This isn't tobacco. You want some?"

I protested, asking them once again to put out their dope. They were so engrossed in each other that they didn't even hear me. Then the young lady rolled down the window and flicked her lit butt into the dry bushes along side of the road.

That action sent me over the edge. I stopped the truck and ordered them out: "Immediately!"

I continued: "I hope I'm making myself clear—you threw that butt out into dry brush. I'm turning the truck around to find it and make sure it's out. You two can do whatever you like, but this is as far as you go with me!"

They just giggled and the fellow said, "We ain't gettin' out, man."

In my youth, I'd been known for dealing with people in very decisive ways. I reverted to my past behavior when I set the truck's emergency brake, took the key out of the ignition, opened my door, stepped around to the passenger side of the truck and opened their door. I grabbed the packs off their laps and threw them into the trees announcing: "You can do whatever you like, stay in the truck and ride with me, but your belongings are staying here for good. Do you get it?"

"Hey, man, you can't do that."

"Well," I said, "It seems I just did. I think your pack was lighter than hers—I think it went over a tree out there somewhere behind the bushes. Too bad."

"You son of a ...," was followed by many more expletives.

My mission accomplished, they did get out of the truck to find their belongings. I hopped in and locked the doors behind me. They hardly noticed me pull away because they were in search of their prized possessions. I turned the truck around and went back to where the butt had flown out. I searched the underbrush and found no sign of any flames. As I passed the two on the road, I could see they were still foraging in the bushes. The young couple "waved" to me in a very disrespectful way. I smiled and waved back.

I drove away, but kept rethinking what had just happened. I always try to help the people I encounter. I am basically a loving and accepting person. But this time it seemed as though in order to help, I had to hurt. They were not getting the message of respect and acceptance I was trying to offer. They abused my efforts. And now I actually had a sense of satisfaction at being an old decisive man of action!

CHAPTER 6

Twelve hours later I was still bumping along the road. The bright sun was creeping into dusk and according to the signs Denver was only about an hour away.

Jack had given unclear directions to his cousin's house. I had a name, Maury, and a phone number. He said that's all I really needed if I were a real truck driver.

I stopped for gas and called the number. Maury's wife gave me some fairly obscure directions, which got me very lost. About dark, I stopped again and with this call I got Maury himself. When I described where I was, he offered to come meet me and guide me to his house.

I waited about ten minutes and there he was. Greeting me with a warm smile and a handshake he said, "I'm Maury, you must be the old man Jack told me about. Why don't you get back in that old truck and follow me to my house. You must be a little tired after such a long drive. My wife has supper ready."

With that he jumped into his pickup and I followed him through the now dark roads. Ten minutes later we pulled up in front of his house. Light poured from the door as his wife, Judy, came out to greet us. She welcomed me inside and introduced me to her two children. Sam, a brown haired boy of about twelve was good looking like his dad and sported some great cowboy boots on his feet. Sara, about fourteen, looked a lot like her mom with straight brown hair.

The children were as pleasant as their parents. We all sat down to the dinner table and conversation turned toward the family's activities. Maury offered, "Judy and I and the kids work in a family shelter downtown on Wednesday nights helping give bedding to the residents."

I asked how they happened to get started volunteering as a family and Judy said: "My mom and dad died several years ago and they had always done volunteer work. We decided to do the same for our family and keep the tradition. We really love it and wouldn't have it any other way. After a while our kids just got used to the idea of helping the poor. They remind us when it's Wednesday night."

I thought to myself that these people were truly loving people —the kind of people the U.S. is made of. Aloud I said, "I drove by the shelter earlier."

"Too bad you weren't here a couple of hours earlier," said Maury. "It's Bible Study night. You would have been able to come with us. We all go. We really like it and the community of people we have met."

I was surprised by the generosity of spirit I saw in this family. I felt a rush of warmth and love flow through me. "I would have enjoyed that," I said. "Perhaps next time."

Exhaustion crept in so I asked if we could hold further conversation until morning. Maury, also tired, readily agreed. I went out to the truck, lowered the tailgate and rolled out my sleeping bag. I loved meeting such good people. As I lay on my bedroll I kept thinking of how Judy's parents had been such an influence in her life and now in the life of her family. I couldn't help thinking of my own children and our many trips to the Tohono O'Odham Reservation in Arizona. Times when I saw poverty through their eyes as they realized the kids on the reservation didn't have the comforts we enjoyed in our home—no running water or electricity or indoor bathrooms or refrigerators. Thinking myself into unconsciousness, I slept like the dead.

I awoke to a gentle tapping on the side of the truck and Judy's soft voice. It was very dark, but the smell of coffee and bacon filled the air. It was morning. "Oh, that smells really good," I said.

"You're welcome to come in and have breakfast when you're a little more awake." Judy said cheerfully. She turned, wearing her plaid robe and fuzzy pink slippers and glided back toward the house. "Maury is at the table reading the paper and having a cup of coffee. Take your time."

Sleeping on the hard wood of the truck bed had caused my left arm to go to sleep. Slowly I uncurled my body and stretched my arms toward the roof of the van. A good yawn got my heart pumping as I threw my legs over the tailgate and jumped down. I saw Judy had left me a cup of coffee. I picked it up and carried it into the house to join Maury. He smiled as I approached.

"Hi again," said Judy from her position in front of the sink.

Maury chimed in, "Now we can introduce ourselves properly. Let's have some breakfast."

They were so inviting that I felt I had known them forever. They made me feel like a favored relative. "Your coffee is good, Judy," I said.

"Thanks," she replied with a wry little smile. "Actually Maury makes it—he gets up earlier than anyone around here."

"Yes," said Maury. "We are early risers and we do enjoy our coffee."

I commented on getting lost the night before. "I always thought I had a better sense of direction than I displayed last night," I said. "Sorry for you having to come and get me."

"Oh, that's okay," Maury answered. Then getting directly to business, he asked, "You don't want to go back to Oregon. Is that right?"

"That's right," I said. "Why do you ask?"

"I was wondering what direction you'd like to go—now that you're here."

I told him that my preferences were either the East or the Deep South.

"Well, that's pretty much what Jack told me. So, I do have a job for you if you would like to drive a fully loaded bobtail to Mobile, Alabama. Jack and I have had a long time dream of expanding our moving company. This is the first time we've ever really had a chance to take action on the dream. Judy and I have prayed a lot and Jack finally said yes. Judy and I believe that you are the answer to our prayers and so we took a contract to move a family whose employer is paying to move them to the South. Jack told us you were a good driver and we like you too. So, you'll be our first driver to go south—that is—if you want the job!"

Of course I wanted the job! I could hardly contain my excitement! "What an honor," I said. "Thanks so much for your trust and the chance to do this for you. I can't thank you enough."

Maury's gentle reply was, "Just finish your breakfast. Judy cooked it specially for you."

As I enjoyed my meal, Maury read the paper and Judy finished the dishes. I savored being with such wonderful people.

So, it was settled. Maury gave me the time and place to meet the crew in Mobile. He also gave me a phone number to call in advance of my arrival so the unloading crew would be alerted. Then he gave me a set of "official" papers and a handsome amount of cash—way more than I expected or thought I deserved —but I did not protest.

We talked a few more minutes about this new business adventure. He talked about how he, Maury, would handle public relations and Jack would coordinate the details and new job contracts. They intended to start small and, with referrals, to increase the workload and their business. I liked thinking I was on the ground floor of this operation and told Maury, "I know you and Jack are going to make it!"

Maury replied, "Jack doesn't know it yet, but I'm going to give you a little bonus if you get the truck to Mobile in one piece, okay?"

I was thrilled and repeated, "Okay!"

Maury continued, "We're going to start loading the truck this morning at seven o'clock and it shouldn't take more than three hours. You can leave as soon as we're finished—probably noon at the latest." (I had forgotten how early we'd all gotten up—it seemed like the middle of the afternoon and it wasn't even 7:00 a.m.)

Promptly at 6:45 a.m. Maury's kids piled into his pickup truck. I followed close behind in the bobtail. We arrived at the customer's house and found all the small items had been boxed and labeled which made for easy loading. Maury was right about the time it took to load—almost to the exact minute. So after three hours with sweat pouring off us, we shut the back door to the truck and I let my excitement spill all over.

"I think I'll leave now," I said. "I don't want any grass to grow under my feet, so to speak."

Judy was very happy that I was so eager to drive the truck. She said, "You know, if you weren't here, Maury would have to drive to Mobile. He asked lots of people about driving, but they all wanted to go west. He just couldn't find anyone who wanted to go east. You are a real Godsend."

I hopped back into the truck carrying the bag lunch Judy had prepared. I was ready to go! I thought, let's get the next leg of this journey started!

CHAPTER 7

Miles passed. It was pure enjoyment. The truck tires crunched over the loose gravel in the first rest stop that was on the border of Kansas. I stopped the truck and opened the bag with my lunch. As I devoured the turkey and cheese sandwich I kept thinking about Maury and Judy—what loving people they were and how thankful I was to have this job!

I opened the envelope containing the important papers and found the map Maury had marked for me. He had not only marked the route, but also had made notes of the places to avoid —some of the less than honorable establishments where people might take advantage of a poor old man from California.

It struck me what a risk Jack and Maury were taking with me. They trusted me to take someone's very special personal belongings all the way across the USA. They hardly knew me and yet they seemed to know I would do my best to make this work—I wouldn't just drive off and sell what was in the truck for my own gain. I wouldn't take precious time taking side trips along the way. They knew in their hearts that I would get this load to Mobile intact. I was determined to live up to their trust.

Pulling out of the Kansas rest stop, I was excited about the 1500 miles that lay ahead of me. I must say I felt a twinge of guilt because I love to drive and I love to see this amazing country of ours. It felt like they were paying me for the privilege of having fun.

"This isn't really what I call being homeless," I mused. "I wonder when things are going to get difficult?" Then I went on, "Just enjoy the moment, Old Man."

Providence (God) had certainly been smiling on me. It was time to accept this gift and move on. Driving, I continued my mental journey through portraits of the faces of friends and loved ones that appeared in my mind.

I thought of Paula who lives on the side of a very steep and dusty hill outside of Tijuana, Mexico. Paula had at one time come to the U.S. to live, but then had returned to Tijuana. When I asked her why she came back to Mexico, she simply replied: "I felt like I was in jail in the United States." Indeed, she has her own life in Tijuana with family and friends. She is very poor, but very happy.

Anyway, when I told Paula that I was going to be homeless for a period of time she said, "You're going to come home dirty and skinny."

I laughed at that prospect. Paula's comment did cause me to pay close attention to my appearance while I was homeless. I am a large man and I knew that I needed to keep clean. I tried to shave each day—sometimes that proved to be a difficult task, but I tried.

Thoughts of Paula faded as I looked at the gas gauge—it was time to fill up. I pulled over into the next gas station and after getting the fuel; I went into the bathroom with my overnight kit. I emerged clean-shaven with a freshly scrubbed face. I felt refreshed and ready for the next few hundred miles.

Before starting the truck I desperately needed to clean the windshield. I grabbed one squeegee from the bucket and at the same time the lady who was parked next to me also grabbed a squeegee. But she dropped hers.

I had glimpsed her from the corner of my eye and it had registered somewhere in my brain that her pants were really tight. So when the squeegee hit the ground, I knew she'd have a hard time picking it up—if she had to bend over. Well, bend over she did and rrrrippp went her pants! They split right up the middle. Smiling at me she ran off toward the restroom. Still smiling she returned with her pants in her hand and her very large sweater pulled way down over her hips. She walked into the office to pay the station attendant and returned to her car still wearing little more than that big smile!

Back in the truck, I drove the remaining daylight hours through mile after mile of wheat fields. I could see forever. The sunset glowed as I approached Oklahoma City. Bright lights decorated dingy storefronts. I had been here 30 years ago. My first and last visit had been when I was a musician in a '60s group called "We Five." We had played to a crowd of nearly 8,000 people as the opening act to the "Righteous Brothers." Today it seemed like another lifetime. However, I had the same tired feeling of being dazed from travel. My memories were replaced by the need to find a place to sleep. I also felt a need to pray. What an incredible journey this had become!

I stopped in a gas station and asked the attendant where the nearest Catholic Church was located. "You got me, buddy, I ain't been to church in years. Try the phone book."

I filled up the truck with diesel and headed to the phone booth. I found mass times listed for St. Anne's on Clover Street. "Do you know where that is?" I asked him.

He shook his head, no.

I never did find a church that night. My desire to sit in a church with my thoughts of gratitude and wonder was short circuited when a storm began to dump rain on the pavement around me. I just wanted to go to bed.

I found a cheap motel and used my imagination to take me into the House of God. I fell asleep with the Gideon Bible on my chest. The last passage I remember reading was from Judges: "But the Spirit of the Lord came upon Gideon, and he blew a trumpet…"

Throughout the night, I woke intermittently to the comforting sound of thunder. From the time when I was a small child, I have always loved the flash of lightning and crashing sound of thunder on warm summer evenings. It gives me the kind of excited feeling that some kids get from going to Disneyland. It's my own personal light and sound show!

I awoke in the morning to the clean air and fresh smell of the earth after a good rain. When I went out to the truck I saw I had parked the truck on a slight incline. Some water had seeped into the back of the truck soaking my personal belongings. Refusing to have my spirits dampened, I decided to wait 'til I got to Mobile to dry out my stuff.

It was 6:00 a.m. and already I was hot and sticky from the humidity that hovered in the 85–95 percentile. I figured it would only get worse as the day went on—and I was right. I felt like I was fully dressed standing in a steam room.

I climbed up into the truck for the day of driving. Even though this was not meant to be a sightseeing adventure, the windshield framed a picture of the countryside that was better than any fine art museum. I liked it so much that I stopped every fifty miles or so to clean the bugs off the windshield so I could continue to enjoy this unexpected blessing of scenery.

I drove for miles without seeing any signs indicating where I was except that I was encountering rolling hills and green grass. Finally I saw a sign reading: "Welcome to Texas." The gentle up and down of the road following the ebb and flow of the landscape tempted me to roll down the window of my air-conditioned truck only to be blasted by the overpowering heat. It was 9:45 a.m. and hot, hot, hot. I wondered if the rest of the South was going to be this beautiful and this hot!

There were lots of road signs advertising historic monuments. I couldn't resist the one in Huntsville where it beckoned: "Home of Sam Houston. Come visit the Sam Houston Museum." It was a ways off the interstate, but I decided to do it. I followed the signs into a parking lot, turned off the truck and went on tour. It was great. Afterwards I relaxed on the warm grass in front of the mansion. The heat made me very tired and I lay back and chewed on a sprig of grass. I fancied myself as Sam Houston might have when he was a boy—just lying there, relaxing on a hot summer afternoon—a real Huck Finn moment.

The time came too soon to move on from this gorgeous spot and continue on my real journey. There were people expecting me. I held on to that memory of lazing in the sun as I drove on to Mobile. In my imaginary life I thought I might give myself a Native American name: something warrior-like—perhaps "Middle-Aged Man Having Mid-Life Crisis." Just a passing thought.

I thought also of my wife, Sue, who had asked me to call once a week—just so she could share in what I was experiencing (and know I was still alive). Tomorrow was my day to call. I wondered how I could explain the experiences of beauty and the kinds of feelings I was having without sounding gushy. How could I tell her about the exhilaration of freedom without making her think I might not want to come home? I thought it would be difficult, but Sue would understand.

Nearing Mobile, Alabama that night, I slept on the gravel under the truck near the side of the road. It was surprisingly comfortable. The night sounds of crickets, small animals and the occasional car or truck passing by soothed me into sleep.

I awoke early—about 4:00 a.m. I was eager to start the day. I rolled out of my moist sleeping bag, packed away my gear and was on the road again.

This was the last leg of my journey as a truck driver. Everything about the trip so far had been spectacular! From the glorious sunrises and sunsets to the colors of plant life exploding around me. The sights, sounds and smells of the grasses and flowers in the countryside had put a spell on me.

Driving through the Alabama countryside, I dreamed that someday Sue and I could move here. Maybe we could even convince our family to move with us! I knew that moving away from our children and grandchildren probably was not an option we would choose. The San Francisco Bay Area was our home. But I could dream. I would recall with my vivid imagination, this time and place. It was so beautiful that it defied description. I sure have no words to describe the awesome effect it had on me. It was incredible.

CHAPTER 8

I made another stop for gas—another stop for dinner. It was another day in paradise. The striking Alabama dusk approached along the Hall's Mill River—just on the outskirts of Mobile. It was a little late to call my contact and a little early to settle in for the night. The call of a hot shower, a soft bed and a rented movie was mighty appealing. I started my search for a room with a view. I felt like it was time for a bit nicer place where I could enjoy myself for the next week or so. Of course I was just dreaming again.

I passed through old sections of town where all the buildings were made of red brick. Then I came to newer sections where some of the buildings were made of stucco with chain link fences. I found Government Street where I knew I needed to be the next morning to meet my helpers. I wanted to familiarize myself with the area so I would not be late in the morning. Turning a corner, I found myself in front of the Greyhound Bus station. This was a pretty rundown part of town. "Whoo-ee!" I said to myself. "I think I've arrived—this is 'Sleeze City South' in all its not-so-glorious glory!"

There was a parking space just big enough for the truck next to a motel sign advertising room prices of $14.00 per night. I parked, climbed down to the ground and on shaky knees from long hours of driving I stood and soaked up the ambiance of the neighborhood. There were two men standing next to my parking space who had a huge paper bag that they were passing back and forth. It apparently contained something to drink, because they were alternately putting it up to their mouths. I walked past and greeted them with "Good evening."

I got a blank stare from one man and the other ignored me as he savored every sip of the liquid in the bag. Passing them, I entered the front door of the hotel. The mustached, red-eyed East Indian woman at the front desk sat behind a window of bullet-proof glass.

Without looking at me, she emphatically stated, "Cash Only! NO women!"

Then she grabbed my $14.00 from the tray that was under the glass and passed back a room key.

The 12 x 12 foot room had a strong urine odor. I discovered some clothes hangers, a shower and a toilet in the closet. The telephone was out of order. Upon further inspection I found the in-house communication worked—so I could get a wake up call from downstairs. The TV looked fine, but was without an electric cord. There would be no movies for me this night. The shower had no hot water, but the non-air-conditioned room was so hot, the cold shower felt darned good.

After showering I went downstairs and asked the desk clerk where I might find a place to eat. She informed me that: "It's ten o'clock at night. There's nothing open but the Burger King at the bus station. I wouldn't walk over there though. There are too many men who want your money and will take it from you if you're out there this late at night."

I thanked her for her advice and headed out on foot to find my burger and fries. I managed to get back to my room with my food and dined on my bed before falling into the pillow. I was remembering Paula's comment about coming back dirty and skinny. I had eaten so much fast food so far on this trip that I was beginning to think I would go home dirty and plump!

Lying on the bed, I stared at the ceiling, meditating on the beautiful day and breathtaking scenery I had enjoyed along the drive. What a great gift it had been. I consciously hoped I would remember my dreams this night because I was expecting a dream of importance about the direction I was to take from here.

But my dreams did not remain with me in the morning because after so many hours of driving, a belly full of French fries and other assorted grease and my tepid shower; I fell sound asleep —my mind on "off."

When my 6:00 a.m. wake-up call jangled me out of my sound sleep I had no idea where I was. For a moment I had visions of having been hijacked into slavery and of being held captive in a tramp steamer destined for far away places. The room was even grosser in the morning light.

Almost immediately, I got up and dressed because it was my day to call Sue. It was really exciting to hear her wonderful comforting voice. I tried to describe my experiences for her. I went on and on about all the little details I could remember. After talking with her, I called my daughter, Julie. I knew she would worry about me, so I made a point of calling her often as the weeks went by. (One of my best investments was a calling card.) I enjoyed every second of my calls to home and family. I've always loved my family, but they took on a special significance over the days and weeks. Often it would be their memory that would sustain me during some of the hard times of my journey.

Ready to go to work, I called my contact in Mobile, Curtis, who informed me that the delivery address had changed. Good thing I called!

At 9:00 a.m. I drove to the newly acquired address and saw three men standing outside the house. The front door was open and the front yard was littered with boxes that the family had brought in their car from Denver.

"Hi there," I called. "Which one of you gentlemen is Curtis?"

"I'm Curtis."

Curtis was a black man about 6'7" tall with huge muscles glistening with sweat. He looked like he was about 45 years old. His crooked nose and cauliflower ears spoke of years of fights. He had a "don't mess with me" look. He showed me where to park the van and told me to get ready for some moving.

Curtis took command of the situation with the precision of a general. His helpers respected his commands and responded immediately. I was not used to the heat and had to take frequent water breaks. Work like this could cause dehydration very quickly. Perspiration poured from me and my clothes were drenched to the point of sloshing. The older of the two workers suggested that I rest while he plodded along at his own even slow gait. He was about my age, but he accomplished the job without so much as a swallow of water. (He was the picture of economy of motion with his slow deliberate movements.)

"How do you keep working in this heat without drinking anything?" I asked.

Both men just kept on working as though I had not spoken a word. Then they both looked at me with a look that said, "Get back to work and quit asking questions."

I knew better than to ask again. I got back to work when Curtis accused me with: "We must be a lot younger than yo, ol fella. Yo sure work slow."

I thought I would be wise to just smile and keep moving.

Water breaks and all, the unloading was done by noon. The cleanup took another fifteen minutes. The new owner of the house was really pleased with our work. He announced, "My wife cooked some fried chicken for ya'll for supper. We also have some lemonade and potato salad."

His wife came outside with the food and set it out on an old hand made quilt that was spread out on the ground. They were a very generous couple and obviously happy to be in their new home.

"You all did such a good job unloading and cleaning up and you did it in such a short amount of time. I'd like to give you a little extra for your good work."

The other men didn't show any reaction to the homeowner's pleasure, but I knew they were thrilled to be getting a bonus. Curtis gave me a disapproving look as he accepted the envelope. Then in a loud voice he proclaimed for all to hear, "This money (five $20.00 bills were in the envelope) is for my workers, not for this old man."

I have a pretty thick skin when I am being insulted—even if it is in front of a group of people. It was clear that Curtis was going out of his way to be mean. I was okay with the distribution of the wealth.

Curtis didn't understand my non-reaction to his insult so he tried one more time. "So my friend in Denver says yo is a tramp. Is tha right?"

I knew that Maury would never have said that.

Without waiting for an answer, Curtis continued, "Me and my friends ain't never been out of Alabama and here yo comes, jes a no good tramp. But 'cause yo white, yo gets yo sef a job drivin a truck all the way from Denver, Colorado. How do yo figur fer that?"

By now everyone had stopped what they were doing to watch my reaction. I took a bite of the fried chicken and with my mouth half full I answered, "Well, I guess I was just in the right place at the right time. I figure I'm just doing what's right for me, Curtis. I think that's all any of us can do."

A few of Curtis' friends had joined our party in front of the house. A few men agreed with me by a slight nod of their heads.

Others stood stooped over and showed no reaction. It was apparent that most people didn't talk back to Curtis.

Later, when Curtis and I stood by the cab of the newly emptied truck, he got up close and spoke directly into my face, "Gimme the keys. You're on your own, Old Man. I don't like you and I don't much like white folks. Haven't met any that I like."

When I didn't respond, he followed with, "I like Maury, though, and I guess I should tell you what he really said to me about you. He said you was a hard workin' coot and that if you ever made it back to Colorado, he'd hire you right away." He went on, "But I ain't gonna hire you no more, cause he left that up to me."

"Well, I guess that means you're finished with me then," I said.

"No, not quite." He reached into his pocket and pulled out one of the twenties and handed it to me. "Get yer stuff out of the cab. Now I'm finished with ya."

I decided to risk stating what was on my mind: "I really don't know how I got onto your deadbeat list, but I do respect your honesty."

Curtis turned, climbed silently into the truck, started the engine and backed it down the driveway. He didn't look back. I knew I'd never see him again. I couldn't help but think that if we had met under different circumstances that we might have become friends.

Curtis

70

PART
II

CHAPTER 9

I stood in front of the house, drenched in perspiration. I knew that the fun was about to start. I was flush with money from my job as a driver. I had no time frame, no one to answer to or any particular place to go. "Pretty nice," I thought.

With Curtis' departure went all my obligations. I was free—really free. Free of any job, free of anything that might keep me down. I was ready to go! I lifted my backpack over my shoulder as an unexpectedly heavy rain began to fall. Quickly I was soaked to the skin. The rain was warm and refreshing after the sweat that had stuck to my skin. I darted from the shelter of one tree to another. With no sun to guide me, I had no idea what direction I was going. I just got onto a long road and started walking.

At that moment I felt like Forest Gump. "Life really is like a box of chocolates, you never really know what you're going to get."

I decided the secret to this situation was to "let go and let God."

After many miles and several hours the rain subsided. Once again I found myself in beauty beyond description. Every thing was wet and clean—no trace of the dry California dust I was used to in the summer. I was pretty sure by the direction of the sun that I was traveling north. I had ventured off the main highway and was walking on a long straight unpaved road that took me into the woods. I was in no hurry so getting lost was more of an adventure than an inconvenience. The newly sunlit day cast shadows across the road for as far as I could see. In the distance there appeared to be some buildings at an intersection. Reaching that point I saw that it was paved for a few hundred yards in both directions across my path. Each of the four corners had it's own attraction. There was a tractor sales yard on the near left corner, a feed and fuel stop across from it on the far left, a dilapidated restaurant on the far right and a fallow field next to me.

A rusty metal sign saying "Eatery" hung from over the entrance to the restaurant. In front of the building was a rust-colored 1949 one-ton Chevy truck that had been modified into a tow truck. I thought I'd stop and eat and just maybe get a ride. I walked slowly and carefully up the creaky wooden steps into the diner.

The only customer was at the counter nursing a cup of coffee. Country music played on a 50's style jukebox. There were unframed 8 x 10 glossy photos with unfamiliar autographs randomly thumb tacked to the walls. At the counter were four ancient red naugahyde covered stools—the kind kids love to spin on. It seemed that the lonely man at the counter was the driver of the old truck outside.

"What'll you have, mister?" asked the friendly proprietor, a man in his early fifties, heavily built with a bald round head.

"A turkey and swiss cheese sandwich, please. Oh, and a cup of coffee, black." (This was my on-the-road comfort food that I ordered whenever I could.)

The coffee was brought out immediately. Then the man turned and happily set to work making the sandwich. All the time he talked to the truck driver, interrupting his chatter long enough to ask if I wanted lettuce and mayo on my sandwich.

"Where ya from?" asked my counter-mate.

"I started off in Oregon about a week ago. Where are you going with that truck?" I decided to get straight to the point.

"I got a call from up north, near the state line," he answered. (I wasn't quite sure what state line he was talking about.)

The sandwich and the bill arrived at the same time. The owner hovered near me until he saw the money. I paid for my meal and took a quick bite, which I complimented. "Hey, this is a really good sandwich."

Turning to the truck driver, I said, "I'm in need of a ride as far north as you can take me. That is, if you don't mind some company."

He told me he could use the company and would be happy to take me as far as he was going. There was very little talk until we both finished our meals.

The truck driver got up from his stool and called out to the man behind the counter: "See ya next time, Flynn."

I added my own goodbye and thanks and followed him out the door. I dragged my backpack behind me and then threw it in the back of the truck—careful to keep it out of the grease and away from the hoist.

"So what brings you way out here in the rain?" asked the nameless driver.

I gave him a short rundown on how I had gotten a job driving from Oregon to Mobile, Alabama. I went on with how much I loved the South. That was just enough to satisfy his curiosity and so it was the end of our conversation. He didn't seem to want to talk or to listen. So I just shut my mouth.

We drove for a time—seemed like about an hour—on dirt roads all the way to God knows where. We saw a few farm animals and lots of black oak trees covered with Spanish moss. It was just the sort of scenery I had anticipated would be in the Deep South.

I broke the silence because I had to comment on the scenery. "I like the look of the Spanish moss on the oak trees here. Months ago I was trying to remember how beautiful this country is, but nothing matches being here. By the way, where are we exactly?"

The driver didn't seem to know quite where he was, but he also didn't reply to my question. I thought he was probably traveling by landmarks that he must know. He just kept on driving.

After about two more hours on the alternately muddy and dusty Alabama dirt road he stopped the truck. We were in the middle of nowhere. He calmly stated, "This is as far as I can take you, mister. My turn is just up the road a ways."

I got out of the cab and went to get my backpack. Coming around to the driver's side I reached out to shake hands. He continued, "Now, don'tcha forget. Walk about a couple a miles and look for the river. When you get to the bridge, turn right and that'll putcha on the road to git a good ride fer yerself. Got it?"

"Yeah, I think so."

He gave me a look that I interpreted to be kind of a sly snigger—like he knew something I didn't. The truck vanished over the horizon of a low hill about a mile away. I was really alone now. I began to walk. This was becoming a very long road.

Looking up at the sky, I saw rain clouds starting to release their treasure on the landscape. I searched for shelter, but found only the black oak trees with their Spanish moss. Soon the rain poured down. My pack just got heavier as I looked for a kind of dry place to set it down.

Just off the road, there was a soft-looking pad of beautiful green grass under one of the trees that was inviting me to sit and rest my weary bones. I aimed what was left of my energy towards the spot under the tree but soon found myself ankle deep in mud. The gooey dark ooze grabbed my feet as if they were stuck in concrete. I teetered back and forth trying not to fall, but I was falling. I let myself go and tipped back wedging my backpack between a rather large rock and the tree. The space was so tight that I had a hard time moving at all. I was starting to have a serious pity party

Stuck in the mud

when I was hit smack dab in the center of my forehead and between my eyes by a soggy piece of dinner-plate-size Spanish moss. In this context, the Spanish moss lost its beauty and allure.

The whole incident took only a few seconds and the pity party became a great belly laugh! I slowly and with great difficulty separated myself from my backpack so I could stand up. Then I decided I might as well enjoy the rain and wait out the storm. I figured later I could wash out my muddy stuff in the river.

When the rain stopped, I walked in the direction that the driver had said I'd find the river. Once there I washed the mud off my soiled clothes and myself. The song in my head went from the usual *"If you want to live life free, take your time go slowly."* To a song from *Carousel:* *"When you walk through a storm, hold your head up high."*

From where I was on the riverbank, I could see another welcoming patch of grass that seemed to be drying in the blistering sun. I walked over and laid out my clothing on the grass where I thought it would probably be dry before nightfall.

As I knelt there flattening my clothes, I also took time to pray with my arms outstretched toward the sun. My time with the Lord over, the river beckoned me. I felt a symbolic rebirth as I jumped into the cool refreshing current. It felt so good with the flow of the cool water around me.

I spent the rest of the day relaxing on the grass by my clothes. Nighttime was equally glorious. As I watched the reflection of the moon on the smooth surface of a nearby river-fed lagoon, an army of fireflies lit up my little portion of the night sky. Their pulsing tails showed color ranging from off white to amber while they darted in and out of the tall grass that lined the water's edge. They flew around like little sparklers on the fourth of July—becoming fuzzier on the dark background until they hypnotized me into a deep sleep.

I was awakened gradually out of my dreams as the sun rose and shone through the saw-tooth outline of the trees on the other side of the water. The memory of my dream was very clear. I had had a similar dream about a year earlier. The setting was St. Peter's Basilica in Rome:

I was a small child, perhaps two or three years old. My hair was snow white. Two people were holding my hands, one on my left, one on my right. We were in a crowd of people packed so tightly around us that it was difficult for me to see more than the legs of the people who were holding my hands—I couldn't see who they were. I couldn't see anything, but I was curious to see everything around me. In immediate response to my desire came action. I began to rise above the heads of the others in the crowd.

As I rise above the crowd I see I am at St. Peter's. The people in the crowd are wearing brilliantly colored gowns from their native countries. The vestments of the priests, bishops and cardinals are the same glowing brilliant colors reflecting all the colors of the rainbow.

Wanting to see more, I rise even higher. Angelic music surrounds me. The entire congregation of people is enraptured as they join in song. The crowd sways together. There is a Mass being celebrated by priests from every country all over the world.

I rise higher and higher and my scope of vision continues to increase. The walls of St. Peter's Square confine me no longer. The people holding my hands begin to take on definition and I see they are very beautiful. I drift so high that the people on the ground are now just a movement of colors. Indistinguishable now as individuals, all I can recognize is the bright rainbow of the world's colors.

From the greatest heights, I can see the curvature of the earth. No walls anywhere and the whole world is bright and brilliant with color.

As though rolling over in bed, I turn over and look skyward to see a dark velvet sky with pinpricks of starlight. All the stars in heaven come together in a bright blue/white set of starlit numbers reading 2004–2014.

Although I had awakened from my dream in the pre-dawn hours, I felt no need to go back to sleep. I wondered about my dream, but I just let it go. I'd dreamt enough in my life to know that the meaning of dreams was often revealed at a later time. The remnant of the warm night contained a symphony of sounds from the buzzing of insects and bellowing of frogs to the pitter-patter of little mammals scurrying from one place to another. An occasional bird chirped to announce the coming dawn.

I rolled out of my sleeping bag and picked up my belongings along with lots of junk left by others prior to my arrival. I couldn't tell which direction I was walking because the clouds had returned covering the morning sun. I could go in any direction. I was free. The fragrant smells of the morning were all around me preventing me from feeling lonely even though I was physically alone. I felt good.

I walked alongside of the river into the morning. After a while the clouds dissipated and the sun shone down in all its hot brilliance. I filled up my water bottles in the water running alongside the muddy slopes of the dirt road. I kept on walking.

A few minutes later a beat up 1942 Dodge pickup truck drove slowly past me and stopped a few feet in front of where I was. I went up to it and leaned into the open passenger side window to greet an elderly woman and a man who was even older and more beat up than the truck. The couple just stared at me until I said, "Thanks for stopping. I was beginning to think I was going to have to walk all the way to Georgia."

The old lady leaned over and whispered something to the driver. Then he turned to me and said, "We're going to Foley. Ya wanna go there?"

I had no idea where Foley was and I didn't much care. Since their pickup was moving in the same direction I was walking, I

A ride with the old folks down a long country road.

just figured I could take off my backpack and kick up my feet for a while.

The old guy said, "Put your stuff in the back. Watch out for the mess. Climb in the bed and hang on tight—we're goin to be in a hurry."

The truck bed smelled like chicken manure and fresh straw. I liked resting on the straw with the gentle breeze and the smell of the country moving past me. In a little while we hit our top speed —about twenty miles an hour. I had no need to go faster. I had no one to answer to when I got to wherever I was headed. I felt like an old dog—sniffing the passing breeze.

Again in the afternoon the sky filled with clouds. This time I was prepared with my poncho, which I had taken from my pack. The rain struck the leaves on the trees and me. It ran down into little pools and then into small streams. The streams turned into rivers and those became waterfalls along side the road. I managed to stay almost dry and could enjoy this brief vision of heaven.

The gentle rain and slow bumpy ride eased us over the bridge and across the river where we were greeted by a "Welcome to Georgia" sign. To me it looked like we were in Mississippi or Louisiana. I was surprised to see so many bayous like I had once seen in Louisiana. I wondered if maybe we were just passing through a corner of Georgia. I loved how this beautiful country of mine was revealing itself to me piece by piece. I really had very little experience in recognizing the flora and fauna of various places.

The road was straight and cut through countryside as beautiful as any I had yet seen. The sight of the sky opening up after the rain had a fairly prehistoric look. There were rotting tree stumps poking through the water on either side of the now one lane road. I figured it would be a real adventure if another car or truck came toward us—cause there sure was no room on either side to move over. Another shower of rain came and went and the brightness of the sun was blinding. The temperature stayed in the mid nineties and the sweat pored out of me as if I were melting. I thanked God for the breeze as we sped down the road.

Riding in the back of the truck, I leaned up against some wire cages that were still embedded with feathers from some long gone birds. Sitting on the straw I picked up some yellowish signatures from those same chickens, who had gone to market. Looking at the mess I was sitting in, I was trying to decide if I was more amused or disgusted. Then the old man yelled back to me, "This is where you get off to get to the interstate."

Gathering my belongings the truck came to a stop and I hopped off. The old fellow drew a map in the air with his finger and then pointed to some imaginary spot that would take me right to where he thought I wanted to go. I thanked him for the ride, told him how much I'd enjoyed it and said goodbye. I reflected on how nice these two old people had been to me. They were pretty cute together too. It wasn't hard to imagine my wife and me like them in a few years.

I walked for a long time until I came to a sign welcoming me to Marysville, a small worn town with no apparent industry. There were lots of people with fishing poles. The pace of life was obviously slow. I loved this! What I saw was a beauty and peace that I could really enjoy. There is a part of small town existence that calls to me in ways that are hard to express with words. It's just a warm content feeling that I get. It felt good to be alive!

This small town atmosphere brought to my mind the summer camp Sue and I had led the previous month in the Arizona desert. We had lived in a small village on the Tohono O'Odham Indian Reservation and worked with the kids from the very small surrounding villages. Memories of that kind of half-speed life filled me as I walked through this lazy town with only my blue baseball cap for cover. Our Arizona summer camp was one of the few activities the Native American kids had during the hot summer days. I was sure that in this town of Marysville, the kids had few if any organized activities. Walking on I thought more about the summer camp in Arizona, the dedication of our counselors, the nights filled with music, prayer and reflection. My memories accompanied me into this small southern town and out the other side into lots of open countryside.

I walked and walked until the sun had set and darkness surrounded me. I had no plan, no idea how far I'd gone or where I'd sleep. It simply didn't matter. My feet were beginning to hurt with every step. I was reminded of the healthy respect due all the people who had walked from place to place throughout history. I could have been living in any century. Except for the paved road and the electric power lines there were so few signs of civilization that I could have been a cave man.

Finally I stopped by the side of the road to camp for the night. I had no campfire or hot food. Cliff bars and water from my backpack tasted really good. I also had a soft sleeping bag and the warm summer air. There was no chance of getting cold. As I lay on the bag in the dark, I heard lots of crunching sounds and critter-like sounds. My curiosity about the sounds lasted only until sleep overcame me. My last conscious thought was, "I wonder if any of the local people have a bicycle they'd like to sell to me?" My feet were getting very tired.

I woke up to discover that my legs were still sore and no one had left me a bicycle. As my mind cleared, I had a feeling of being truly blessed. I had found work that had provided me with money and I had food. So often homeless people have no resources. I thought about how attitude really affects one's approach to life. In my work with homeless people I had seen plenty of people who had food, but could only complain about what they didn't have. Then I also saw people who had nothing, but were so grateful for being alive and being able to take another breath. I really enjoy awakening to philosophical thoughts.

Walking along that morning the song in my head was: "Amazing grace, how sweet the sound, that saved a wretch like me. I once was lost, but now am found, was blind but now I see."

I was trying to "see." That's why I was on this journey. In my work, I had met so many desperate people, who were so alone and so lost. These words coming to me were very timely indeed. Had I not been on this long quest, without an agenda, I might have missed the grace surrounding me in this precious present moment. I was about to meet Thomas.

CHAPTER 10

It was getting unbearably hot, so I stopped walking, took off my backpack and collapsed along side the road. I thought I'd let my "North" sign do the work. I sat on the ground next to an on-ramp to the highway. Exhausted, my eyes closed and I was asleep. I woke some time later and noticed a convenience store across the road. I guessed it must be around nine p.m.

I walked across to the store where there was a Datsun car parked with the driver kind of slumped over the steering wheel. The driver's side door was open and a man's arm was hanging down. I was hungry so I thought I would check him out on my way into the store. Up close he looked like he was sleeping. Deciding I'd not bother him, I went into the store and bought a sandwich and a coke. Passing him again on my way out, he was practically falling onto the ground.

I walked up to the car and said, "Hello" in my usual friendly way. It startled him so that he jerked into an upright position. "Sorry," I said. "Are you having some trouble?"

Fully awake now, he looked at me curiously. He seemed pleased that I had stopped and replied, "No. No trouble, unless you call being late getting home to my wife in Savannah who's ready to deliver our baby, trouble!"

I tried to absorb what he had said. "Wow!" I exclaimed. "This could be good for both of us!"

"What do you mean?" he said.

"Well I'm awake and have a good driving record and I wouldn't mind going to Savannah, Georgia at all. If you are too tired to drive right now, I can get us there and you can rest." (What a sales pitch!)

I continued on, telling him how I had missed the birth of my son Peter (because he was born before I could get the surgical booties required in the delivery room on my big feet). Perhaps that helped him decide I was okay.

"You've sold me," he said with a smile. "Why don't you drive and I'll give you directions."

I got into the driver's seat and looked closely at the young fellow's drawn tired face and bloodshot eyes and I asked, "Have you been traveling a long time?"

Without answering my question, he stated, "My name's Thomas."

It was apparent he was exhausted and I was excited that I had allowed the spirit to guide me to Thomas. He needed help to get home.

He went on, "I've been in Las Cruces, New Mexico on business. I stopped here because my car was overheating. I was also tired and hungry."

"Yes," I said. "I wouldn't be surprised if your car overheated because you were going so fast. You have to be careful in this heat."

"My dad and I are in business together. We have a shop on one of the islands off the coast of Georgia—a heating and air conditioning shop." Thomas' voice faded a little as he sighed and yawned. In a more subdued voice he said, "We're four hours away from Savannah and my wife's already having contractions. I just called her."

"Don't worry, buddy, we'll get you home." I whispered the words very softly as he fell into a deep sleep.

Two hours of driving went by and I needed to make a pit stop. I used the chance to grab coffee and a sweet roll. Thomas never stirred.

Another half hour passed and Thomas' eyes fluttered open and he asked where we were. I had just passed a sign reading "Savannah 108 miles."

Thomas looked at his watch in disbelief. "It's almost one in the morning!"

I told him. "I still have half a cup of coffee left. It's cold, but you're welcome to it if you want."

"Well done! We're almost home. Thanks for driving. I don't know what I would have done if you hadn't come along. Let's pull over at the next station and gas up. I can call my wife then."

That sounded good to me. I stood by the car in the gas station while the attendant filled the tank. Thomas went inside to make his phone call. He came out saying his wife was still in labor and there was no baby yet. He was pretty excited and happy.

"Did I tell you that I made the sale that I went to Las Cruces for? I didn't tell my wife that I have to go back in two weeks for delivery of my design. But she'll be proud."

"No, you didn't tell me. It looks like congratulations are in order. I'm sure your wife will be proud. And I'm sure she understands that you have to travel."

"Yeah," said Thomas. "She won't understand though, if I don't get home for the birth of the baby."

The conversation lightened up as we got closer to Savannah. It was a little after 2:30 in the morning and it looked like he'd make it for the birth of the baby. The last couple of minutes of our time together were spent in prayer for the safe delivery of the baby. We pulled into Savannah and he dropped me by the City Hall next to the Savannah River. I got out of the car. Thomas was coming around from the other side. I turned to shake his hand when he asked my name.

"They call me Old Man."

"Well, thanks, Old Man."

Thomas slipped into the driver's seat and drove away. He was gone before I could raise my hand to wave goodbye. He was on his way home.

"Thomas"

CHAPTER 11

It was late (or early) and I was very tired. Even in the dark I could see some of my surroundings. Savannah was beautiful! The streets were well lighted and the river shimmered with lights from the nearby stores. I knew Savannah was going to be my first real test case in trying to understand the plight of the homeless on a more personal level, because I was going to make an effort to connect with people and soup kitchens and shelters—it was time.

I walked from the riverfront toward the City Hall. I came to General Green Park where there was a large statue of the General himself. It was a beautiful monument with a flat vertical surface on the pedestal just perfect to lean against. My eyes closed as I leaned back and soon I was sound asleep.

Savannah was the most beautiful wake-up call I'd ever had (next to my wife, Sue). "My God," I thought. "I am in fantasy land." Then the heat hit me. I was covered with perspiration. My clothing was soaked down to my socks! The sun's rays were just kissing my forehead in the early morning light.

I'd had a semi-comfortable night's sleep, but I felt exhausted. I dragged my backpack from behind a bush near the General's statue. With a quick glance around me, I clumsily pulled the now very heavy backpack onto my shoulders. I could see scores of homeless people in the park. They were sitting on benches, talking in groups or just leaning against trees. They were seemingly invisible to the tourists passing by.

I stopped just a few feet from where I'd started on the other side of the statue. It hit me. "I am finally anonymous." I sidled over to two gentlemen who looked to be about my age and asked, "I'm new in town. Where can I get a bite to eat and a place to stay?"

The two men stopped their conversation and told me there was a Baptist church that made a pretty good dinner. "They open up at 11:30 a.m. We're going over there. You can follow us if ya' want to."

I thanked them and accepted their offer. "Do either of you have the time?"

Just at that moment a church bell rang out eleven times. "It's eleven."

I discovered the church bells ring on the hour every day of the week in Savannah.

We three wanderers sauntered past at least ten churches on the way to our meal. We arrived just as the line queued up. People were starting to walk inside. The marquee out front read "St John the Baptist Church and listed the mass schedule. I guessed they thought it was a Baptist church because of the name.

They didn't care who was feeding them. They just wanted to eat. I asked, "Why do you think people here want to feed the likes of us?"

It took about half a second for one man to answer gruffly, "It makes them feel good." My two companions disappeared into the crowd.

Once again, in my friendly fashion, I talked to a woman who was standing in line near me—another guest of this soup kitchen. She seemed to be in her early forties. She was unkempt and unwashed. I said, "I think Savannah is one of the most beautiful cities I've ever seen."

She turned to me with a vacant look—almost as if she had heard something, but didn't quite connect that I was speaking to her. She replied, "I wouldn't know, I've lived here all my life."

I was used to working with homeless people who traveled a lot from one place to another—always looking for something different or trying to escape family or situations that put them in some kind of jeopardy. I wanted to ask her more questions, but the line was moving and I lost track of her in the crowd.

Several people were talking among themselves. No one took notice of me. I had wondered if I would stand out in a crowd of homeless, but it seemed I was blending in very well. The people serving took no notice of me, which was good and bad. When I worked with homeless people I tried to pay attention to their needs and wants. I prided myself on my relationships with people —homeless or not. Here in this place, I was almost invisible. No one talked to me. No one looked at me. I had a feeling of real loneliness in this place full of people who were here to feed the likes of me.

It was Saturday and the noon liturgy at Saint John the Baptist Church had let out. Some of the parishioners came from the church over to the dining area. There had been a group let in before me who appeared to have been served breakfast. I was in the first lunchtime group—or dinner as they called it in the South.

People from the church magically appeared in their aprons to greet people at the door. Their greetings were warm and cheerful. The person who greeted me looked into my eyes. But as I went through the food line, I got little more than food on my plate. Again I could have been invisible.

The food was great. The cooks took their job seriously. I wanted to do something in exchange for this meal. So I approached a woman who was serving and said, "Excuse me Ma'am."

"Yes, would you like something more?" she asked.

"No, thank you. The food was very good and there was plenty of it. You are all so nice to do this. I'd like to help you—I can help clean up or serve or whatever you need."

"Oh," said the woman with a surprised look on her face. "Oh, no! You just enjoy your meal and we'll do all the work. That's why we're here."

I tried to convince her that I loved to help—I'd like to pay in some way for what I had received.

"Well," she said in the most beautiful Southern drawl I'd ever heard, "that's not the way we do things around here. You just enjoy your food and if you want more you just let me know. I'll see to it. My name is Martha and I'll be serving you."

She seemed completely unaware of what I was trying to say— that I wanted to participate in the helping community. She smiled at me and turned to leave. She had a spring in her step and went on to serve someone else. She had not even asked me my name.

I sat for a few minutes thinking over this exchange that had just taken place. I was really upset by what she had said and the fact that she wouldn't accept any help from me. I felt useless. I thought again about all the people I had known in my own ministry with the poor. So many men and women who had nothing to do and nowhere they were expected and no one to look out for them. I always thought that a place like a soup kitchen was a place where people could be accepted and welcomed and made to think they were cared about as well as cared for. I felt far from cared about. I felt like I just needed to eat my meal and get out of the way so the volunteers could do what they wanted to do.

Somewhere I had read a quote from Mother Teresa who said something about needing to be human beings not human doings. I guess I was feeling like these volunteers were doing their job, but forgetting to be human and enter into a relationship with someone they perceived to be different from themselves. I wondered why this woman wouldn't let me help. Was she afraid of me? Was she unwilling to give up the work that made her feel good? I suppose she could have had lots of reasons, but I still wondered.

As I watched the volunteers serving and cleaning up it looked to me like a clique of friends doing their "good thing" for the poor. It didn't appear they were doing much with the patrons to increase their self-worth. I also knew that most of the people eating here just wanted to finish their meal and get out. But there were a few like me who would have loved to join the helpers.

I was still thinking about all this when Martha came back to the table. She nicely asked the people to clear out. The message was unspoken but clear: We've done all we are prepared to do for you, now, get out.

After the great meal, I walked across another park toward the rectory of the church. Behind the rectory was a grade school. There were teenagers in the schoolyard playing games with little children. I approached one of the teenagers and asked, "Do you know where there is a homeless shelter?"

He replied, "No, I don't, but the lady at the desk in the rectory would probably be able to help you."

I walked toward the front of the property and was surprised to see a modern looking building in the midst of the traditional brownstone buildings. The front door of the rectory was open so I walked up to the Formica counter. Beyond the counter a young woman was typing. "Excuse me," I said. "I was just talking to the young man watching the children in the yard and he said you might be able to answer a question for me."

"Yes, sir," she said with a smile. "What would you like to know?"

"Do you know of a homeless shelter where a traveler like me can stay overnight?"

"Yes, Sir. Our shelter is on Liberty Street. Do you want directions?"

She handed me a piece of paper with written directions to the shelter and then remarked it was supposed to be her day off. "It's normally quiet on weekends so I can get caught up on my work," she said.

I walked out of the rectory into the afternoon heat. I had misplaced my blue cap somewhere along the way and the heat of the sun beat down on the top of my bald head. I could feel my scalp getting redder and redder. I walked past several parks where homeless people were congregated under trees or cooling themselves in the city fountains.

The heat was so harsh that I decided to do what everyone else was doing. I took off my shoes and backpack and hopped over the two-foot tall wrought iron fence surrounding a fountain. I sat on the edge of the fountain and gratefully dangled my tired aching feet and legs into the cool, bubbling water. The others sitting by the water were laughing and having a good time splashing each other.

After my cool respite at the fountain I thought I would look for the shelter. My feet had cooled, but I decided to take the air-conditioned bus. I made my way to the bus stop near the park and waited a short time. Soon the bus pulled up and I told the driver where I wanted to go. Then I found a seat and looked out the window.

On the bus route we passed several parks. Next to a shopping center was a particularly beautiful park that had a sign reading "Forsythe Park." Between the shopping center and the park I could see a large group of men standing around. They looked like they were waiting for work—for someone to come along and offer them a job for the day.

In my home area of California I was used to seeing men waiting outside the garden centers. Employers would drive by and pick them up to take them to job sites or to their own homes to work. At the end of the day the employer would drive them back to where they'd been picked up and give them their day's wages.

The men I knew who made a living this way worked very hard. Sometimes they would finish a day of hard labor and the employer would take them back to where they had picked them up and just drive away. I knew many men who were left without any money after a long day of backbreaking labor.

"It's your stop, here's where all the bums and drunks hang out," called the driver.

The driver's comment bothered me. I wondered how much of this attitude was going to surround me in this beautiful place.

I silently exited the bus. Looking around me I saw a mass of humanity. "So this is what bums and drunks look like—they look okay to me," I said to myself.

There were so many people trying to get into the shelter that I felt guilty trying to take a place someone else could have. I decided to stay in the park that night. I found what looked like a comfortable place under and behind a bush near another beautiful fountain. All night I heard the sound of the water, the rustle of leaves, crunching of branches and pounding of running feet. Before falling asleep, I thought about my call to Sue the next day. I thought I might call her after church when I was rested and in a happier mood.

It was a short night's sleep. But I woke up with lots of energy to get moving. I rolled up my gear and began my walk to Saint John the Baptist Church. As I neared the church I saw there was a man who appeared to be sleeping on the front steps. People were walking around him as they entered the church. Getting closer I could see he had a long white beard and bushy white hair struggling out from under a hat. He seemed very old and was very dirty. He held in his folded arms a burl-wood type walking stick much like an old fashioned shillelagh. He leaned on this stick as he sat peacefully sleeping.

I decided I would get him a cup of tea. I walked across the street and soon returned with two steaming cups (morning coffee for me). As I approached the steps I could see he was still sleeping. But as I stood watching him and then leaned over to put the cup next to him, his eyes popped open! He was instantly awake. His eyes riveted into mine.

"I brought some tea for you, if you like it?" I said.

I was really startled by his presence and wanted to know more about him. So I quickly followed my first comment with another question. But instead of asking what I intended to ask, "Why are you here?" I blustered, "Why am I here?"

I immediately realized my error, but he answered my question just the way I had asked it. Peacefully, he replied, "We are both here to do the will of God. You are willing to do that?" Before I could answer, he continued, "Accept your gift from God completely. You are willing to do this?"

I was stunned. Chills went through me like electricity. "Yes," I stammered.

The "Guardian"

He said, "You have answered God's call. Now only do that which brings you peace. You will have no fear. God loves you. He loves you as a little child. Accept your gift completely. You are willing to do this?"

This was such a direct and difficult question, but I felt compelled to answer, "Yes!"

I felt like a little child. I was completely transfixed by the wisdom of this dirty, long-bearded little man. I heard myself ask, "Where would you like to go to eat?" (And immediately I thought —why couldn't I find something more profound to say!)

"I eat bread. Do you have bread?" he asked.

I ran across the street down a ways to the market—like a puppy running for a bone! I bought a loaf of sourdough bread and brought it back to the smiling old man. With the bread, the tea and a thank you; the old man got up from the step of the church, gave me a little bow and started to slowly walk away. I was wide-eyed. I wanted to talk all day with this person. Instead, I stood up to say a proper goodbye.

My hand was shaking as I attempted to drink my coffee. I couldn't hold the cup to my mouth. As soon as the man disappeared around the corner of the church I walked the few steps to the corner of the street to find him. But the street and sidewalk were empty! There were a few door stoops and a few open windows, but there was no elderly man to be seen. I couldn't understand how this very slow, very old man could get away so fast.

My hand still shaking, the coffee was burning my skin. I felt faint, light and heavy all at the same time. I felt happy and sad and confused. My coffee was history. What had I just seen? Who had I been talking to? Was I daydreaming? I was totally awake.

"God loves you and he loves the little child in you." Remarkably, I had been thinking just that thought the day before.

It was time for my weekly call to Sue. I told her the story of what had just happened. Then I went on to say that I had this desire to give everything away and live as this old man did.

Sue's simple and direct reply was, "His, is not your calling."

Much later when I had returned home, I talked to my friend, Cricket. She told me that such people had a name in the Russian tradition: "Poustinikki." A poustinik is a person who is called from God to leave everything and enter a desert place in order to pray for the sins of the world. They stay close enough to help and serve others when needed, but live alone, like a hermit, in a secluded place called a "poustinia" which means "desert."

That seemed to be exactly what the man had been doing. I wondered if I should have thrown my backpack into the bushes for some other homeless person and start traveling as this holy man was doing. I knew I lacked the courage to do that. Besides, I also loved my family too much to leave them permanently. And as Sue said, it was not *my* calling.

I was feeling sad. I wondered if it was like the sadness of the young man who asked Jesus, "Lord, what do I have to do to enter the kingdom of heaven?" And Jesus replied, "Go, sell all you own and come follow me." (Luke 18—loose translation)

Courage was not an issue I had really considered before the old man on the church steps had asked me, "You are willing to do this?" To me, courage was defined as "doing something in the face of fear." Even now, I didn't want to admit to myself that there was anything I feared. I felt like I had talked to Christ Himself through the old fellow. So few words were spoken, yet the old man seemed to know who I was in the scheme of God's plan. He seemed to know what was most important—Love. Not the kind of mushy stuff of movies, but the kind of accepting, generous, unconditional love that doesn't judge, but sees each person for who they are.

I thought about the small subtle things that drive people apart —how people belittle each other and somehow drew comfort from making the other person look less than they were. It made me think of Curtis who had tried so hard to put me down.

I had made my way back to the park and I was distracted from my thoughts by a woman, very thin, with long greasy graying black hair whose face kind of caved in around the mouth—like she had no teeth. She wore a sweater over a quilted vest that was buttoned all the way up the front. Her pants were filthy and her shoes were about to fall off because she had no shoelaces. Her hair was held back from her face with a pair of earmuffs—the kind that are used in very cold climates. She had a plastic bag of bread, which she was punching and squeezing with her feeble fingers. She had opened the top of the bag and I thought she was going to feed the birds. Then she reached into the pocket of her ragged pink sweater and brought out a bottle containing some kind of liquid, which she proceeded to pour into the open plastic bag of bread. She continued punching and squeezing the bag until the contents were a kind of mushy consistency. To my surprise, she opened the bag, reached in and grabbed a handful of this stuff and sucked it off her fingers!

As she ate, I eased myself next to her on the park bench. Her face was a mass of crumbs and white paste. I asked if she'd like some coffee.

"No thanks," she answered. "But thanks for asking. That's a lot more than anyone else usually offers."

"Do you live near the park?" I asked.

"No, I take the bus from the senior center—down the road a piece. Too many old people there."

That started a conversation that lasted into early afternoon. I learned what living was like for an elderly woman on a fixed income. She mostly talked about her family who had abandoned her many years before. According to her they had spent all her money and never made an attempt to find out where she was.

In the last few minutes of our conversation she said, "Thank you so much for visiting. I've had a wonderful morning."

"Is there anything I can help you with?" I asked. I was feeling pretty happy at the moment with my new friend.

Before she could reply, a young couple drove past us and they threw balls of wadded up paper in our direction. They yelled out their open windows, "Worthless deadbeats go back where you belong!"

My heart hurt. What had we done to deserve such treatment? I felt especially bad because their comments resounded as such a death knell to the spirit of this beautiful old woman. She was on her feet immediately, moving as far away from me as possible. Our encounter was over.

I was filled with questions. What made that young couple look past our common humanity and address us as less than animals? Where did we belong? What was the "good citizen" mold we did not fit? Where would this kind of attitude stop? Where would we be safe? What would Christ do in this situation?

I shrugged my shoulders and "turned the other cheek." It was really difficult, but I knew I just had to take the bad with the good.

Later that same afternoon, while I was hitchhiking away from the site of the previous incident, two cars stopped near me, pinning me to the side of the road. The occupants got out and, surrounding me, yelled stuff at me about how worthless "my kind" were and how unwelcome we were in "these parts." When I showed no reaction, they got back into their cars and drove off.

I was blessed that none of these guys had become dangerous to my person. I knew that had I become the least bit hostile, the outcome might have been different. That night I sought shelter for more than just my body, my spirit needed some sheltering as well. Savannah had turned out to be a lesson in more than I had anticipated.

CHAPTER 12

I was heading in the general direction of where people had told me there was a shelter called the Potter's House, but in order to prevent further confrontations, I tried to keep to the side streets. Eventually I arrived.

The street was lined with beautiful green trees. The neighborhood looked like it might have been a pretty nice place a few years back. The Potter's House was a green building with peeling paint and trashy exterior. Inside the linoleum made a pattern of large squares.

A man welcomed me and recited the rules (no alcohol or other drugs, no smoking, arrive before 4:00 p.m., each person is allowed about fifteen squares for their bedding, leave by 7:00 a.m.). I was told there were no more vacancies for the night. The person at the front desk recommended another shelter.

I left the Potter's House and tried to follow the directions I'd been given. I wandered for the better part of the evening—lots of walking with a backpack that got real heavy at the end of the day.

Very late that night I was wandering in a pretty rundown part of town. Near the Greyhound station I found another shelter called Grace House. I went up to the door and was greeted by a man who introduced himself as John. I could see he had the use of only one eye—the other was clouded over. He was a kind man who told me his life history—how he had come up the hard way. He'd battled drugs and gang violence. He'd lost the sight in his one eye in a brawl over some bad debts. In between all this he told me about Grace House and what kind of great place it was. He outlined the rules for staying—rules similar to the Potter's House—except they served two meals: dinner at 6:00 p.m. and breakfast at 7:00 a.m. Then he gave me the bad news—no room. He said they seldom had any open spaces. It saddened me, because this seemed like the kind of place I'd like to stay.

Knowing I couldn't stay there, I was curious about the apparent success of this place. I asked, "Why do you think your shelter works so well, John?"

"We love everyone who comes through these doors, that's why."

For the rest of the night, I rode around Savannah on the bus. I was surprised at how tolerant the bus driver was. There were lots of other souls like me riding that night—just looking for a safe place to sleep. My goal was to get off at dawn, find a park to sit and write in my journal and get a bite to eat.

At 7:00 a.m. I had disembarked by the same park with the fountain I had seen three days earlier. I found a café where I had breakfast and headed for the park about 9:30 a.m.

I noticed a playground, which I had not seen on my previous visit. There were about 30 little kids playing. I could see a small merry-go-round and some slides with sand around them. This was a center of noise and action—kids squealing, birds singing and squirrels chattering.

I found a shady spot under a pink-blossomed tree with Spanish moss hanging off the branches. I was inspired by the joyful noises surrounding me and took out my writing pad. I could feel myself relax in this pleasant place when I heard a little voice ask, "What'cha doin?"

Looking up toward the slide, I saw a little boy standing in the bright sun. He was about five years old, barefoot, wearing shorts and a plain t-shirt.

He repeated, "What'cha doin, Mister? Writin?"

"What are you doin here in the park?" I responded. "Playin?"

The boy nodded "yes" and in a child's disjointed conversation stated, "That's my sister over there on the slide. Do you want to know her name?"

"Very much," I answered.

"My sister knows how to sing 'Bingo.' Do you want to hear me sing it?"

"Sure," I said.

"Whatcha eatin? It smells like my dog when it gets wet."

"You're probably smelling me," I stated, "because I'm not very clean."

Satisfied with my honesty, he started singing "Bingo."

Hearing him, his sister scrambled down from the slide and joined in "There was a dog, it had a name, Bingo was it's name, Oh, B-I-N-G-O, B-I-N-G-O, B-I-N-G-O, ohhh Bingo was his name O."

We sang the song together for a very long time and drew a small crowd of other children who joined in the singing with us. Finally the children all lost interest and they returned to their play on the merry-go-round and slides.

Once again, I was alone to do my writing. These small children were so unlike the young people I'd encountered the previous day. I wondered what caused the change in a person—why couldn't we stay like little children—so loving and accepting. I thought about my own children and grandchildren—I was definitely missing them today.

The day passed so quickly that I again missed the time to get into a shelter for the night. I not only missed check in time at the shelter, I missed dinner as well. The kitchen was closed at 5:00 p.m. There were lots of rules about where I could stay and when I

"B-I-N-G-O"

could eat. In many ways it was easier to stay on the street than to find a shelter. I decided my day in the park was worth the hunger and disappointment of not having a place to stay. So I unrolled my bedding right there in the children's playground and quickly fell asleep.

The next morning's awakening was blissful. A thousand bells ringing in every conceivable overtone sang out—obscuring the sounds of traffic. I loved the sound of the bells. It reminded me of Sunday mornings going to church with Grandma. Here in Savannah the bells were a daily ritual.

The next few days I spent in the park, writing in my journal. I was trying to catch the fullness of every moment, every experience. When hunger overcame me, I ate at the nearest McDonald's or Burger King. Sometimes I'd go to the grocery store and get an apple. I didn't like to shop—it took lots of time and I had no place to store or carry much more than what I already had. When sleep overcame me, I slept.

Finally I felt like I'd better not overstay my welcome in the park. It was time to find a place to stay. I left the park and went searching for a place I'd heard many of the other homeless people talking about called Emmaus House.

After exiting the park I wandered in circles most of the day. I came upon a Laundromat so I washed my clothes—boy did they need washing! I sat in the Laundromat watching my clothes go around. It seemed like the rotation of clothing was a surreal movie about my experience so far. Having reached into the bottom of my backpack for all the dirty clothing, I actually found my blue hat. Life was pretty good!

It was then very late in the afternoon when I came out of the Laundromat, and realized I needed to ask directions to Emmaus House. How had I gotten lost again? On the street I found a helpful citizen and was on my way.

I was again too late to get into a shelter. Della met me at the front door of Emmaus House with a pocket watch on a string around her neck and a huge smile on her face. "I'm sorry, sir, you're a little late for entrance into the shelter for the night, but the inner city shelter has openings all night if you don't mind taking the bus across town."

I was thankful for the advice, but opted for a dry spot among the bushes back in the park where I'd spent the last few nights. I headed back in the direction I had come—by a more direct route this time. When I arrived in my old location my spot was already occupied. I had to search for another spot and settled on a bench that was unclaimed. It was mine for the night.

At 7:00 a.m. sharp, I was in the Emmaus House breakfast line. Ushered in to a table, I ate a breakfast that was great by any standard. My server was the kind, accommodating Della. She asked, "Have you met Pastor Steve?"

"No, I haven't. Who is he?" I responded.

She told me that he was the man who made things happen when it came to social justice issues in the city. "If you want to know what's going on here in Savannah, you best ask him. He knows everything!"

It was obvious Della had a real case of hero worship when it came to Pastor Steve.

"How long have you been waiting on people here in the kitchen, Della?"

"Oh, years!" she said with a smile. "Would you like another cup of coffee?"

I could see she was as content as any worker I had ever seen. She served each person with cheerfulness and consideration.

"What keeps you coming back to serve?"

"I haven't missed a day here for six years. I've been serving my whole life, but nothing has been as fun or has given me the sense of doing what is so right as what I'm doing now. I believe that all God's people need to be heard and really listened to, don't you?"

"Yes," I agreed. "But I don't hear it out loud from very many people. It makes me happy to hear it from you."

"Well," she said, "How about it, do you want another cup of coffee?"

I couldn't resist her invitation and accepted the cup of steaming brew. I watched as she poured and then moved on to the next "customer." Della was the kind of behind-the-scenes person who knew everyone. As a woman of roughly 75 years of age, she had seen and heard almost everything. I could see her bending over to listen to each person who had something they wanted to share over their morning coffee. I was sure she was a therapeutic presence in this place—people would know that what they told her was private and confidential. The fact that she'd been working here in one spot for so long was intriguing to me. I knew I was watching a true saint.

Della and Benny in the shelter

Della's final advice to me was to stay in the park across the street so I could get into the Emmaus House shelter when the doors opened at 4:00 p.m. Shortly after four, I found myself inside the shelter. It was clean and well organized by a dedicated staff of volunteers. I was pleasantly surprised to see Pastor Steve at the door welcoming each visitor. He greeted the old timers like they were part of his family entering his home. He seemed to be a man with a huge heart who loved to serve. I prayed silently that God grant me that grace of selfless service.

When it was time to settle in for the night, the smokers trailed in from outside where they were enjoying their last puffs. Along with them came a trail of smoke that filled the room with an inversion layer from about two feet above the floor.

The beds were blue mats issued to each man who then found his place somewhere on the floor. Quickly, the old-timers staked out the best territory. Newcomers like me got what was left over

—the spaces by heavy snorers and the spaces near the high traffic areas. All night long, on my nice soft mat, I heard the sounds of rustling, coughing, snoring and shuffling that kept me on the waking edge of sleep.

Early morning finally dawned and a wonderful woman with a stopwatch hanging from a string around her neck came through and spoke gently, "its 5:30, time to get up." Over and over she went from one end of the hall to the other repeating the refrain. "It's 5:30, time to get up."

Each time she reached the side of the hall where the light switches were located she would flick on another set of lights and speak a little louder. There were some who were still sleeping. Her voice got louder as she attempted to awaken her clientele. She was trying to do her job—get the clients up and out so they could begin breakfast.

I was reminded of my wife Sue's gentle presence on our group trips to Tijuana and the Tohono O'Odham Indian reservation when she would awaken our groups of teenagers before a day of work. The reaction of the homeless men was much the same as the reaction of the teens—"Go away...we're not getting up...leave us alone...." However the gentle but insistent voice wouldn't stop until the last person had rolled out of their respective sack.

Once everyone was awake, our human alarm clock gave instructions about the breakfast being served next door in the hall. This announcement helped the grumpy attitudes a little— very little.

No one was really supervising personal belongings. We had left them in one central space the evening before. I suggested to the soft-spoken woman that they might want to try a "claim check" system. This way no one would be missing anything in the morning. She seemed too busy to even hear my suggestion. She acknowledged my comment with "Oh, that happens all the time."

At about that time I found my backpack in the pile and discovered my jeans were missing—but someone had left a sandwich in the vacant place. I recalled my recent suggestion, wrote it on a piece of paper and put it on her desk and went to breakfast. I hoped she would remember my gentle complaint and do something about this system before more people had missing items.

When breakfast was over I left the dining room. I walked around the corner from the kitchen and discovered a coffee machine, which rewarded me with nothing for the quarter I inserted. I figured I'd lost that one!

I didn't think I'd try to get back to Emmaus House for lunch, so I stopped in a shop to get a sandwich for lunchtime in the park. (I had filed the donated sandwich in the garbage—its age was unknown.)

I got to the park and settled in for a morning of relaxation. A very friendly pair approached me. "My name is Ronnie and this is my old lady, June. We've never seen you around these parts. You passing though?"

"Yes," I said. "I'm trying to find out about all the shelters around here so I don't stay too long at any one place."

Ronnie and June seemed to want to help me. He began to talk to me about all the shelters available. He also counseled me about the need to be on the lookout for thieves.

I wondered why Ronnie and June hadn't found a job. Ronnie talked about hating working with people. He had tried working for a while, but it wasn't for him. Ronnie was very engaging to talk with. June seemed very bright. While Ronnie was entertaining me with stories of his working woes, June was fumbling behind me. I was so attentive to Ronnie, that I wasn't paying attention to her. I was interested in why they endured shelter life.

Ronnie confided in me that he had just gotten out of jail and no one wanted to hire an ex-con. He was resigned to being on the street at this point in his life. June appeared in front of me and announced she was going to find a bathroom and she would be right back. Some time passed and Ronnie excused himself to find June. He told me he would be right back to take me to the shelter they had chosen.

I settled back to enjoy the morning. I had nowhere to go. It was a beautiful day and the birds in the park were singing the day's praises. Fifteen or twenty minutes passed and there was no sign of Ronnie or June. I opened my backpack to get my blue hat to shelter my balding scalp from the rays of the sun. "Damn," I said, discovering that the bottom zipper to my backpack was open. A few things were sticking out. On closer inspection I realized I was missing some money—about $13.00 and a few Cliff bars—nothing too important. I guessed June had been working behind me while Ronnie was entertaining me with his stories.

Con artists are all around, I thought. These two had been extremely professional. Fortunately, they had not gotten much and I sure had learned a valuable lesson.

I went across the street to the Emmaus House dining room and met a much older man than me who had apparently been watching me in the park. "So," he said, "You've been scammed by Ronnie and June. I seen the whole thing. They do that to everyone new. There's not nothin' no one can do about it neither cause no one wants to press charges."

I took a chance by telling Pastor Steve about the incident. Although he was understandably upset, his comment was, "All we can do is pray for them and hope that someday they will become Christians."

Pastor Steve knew there was little that could be done even by the police. This was a neighborhood full of crack houses. The guys who used, often turned to stealing to support their habit. It would take all the local law enforcement resources to identify these houses, let alone arrest the occupants. Drug addiction and substance abuse were common in the neighborhoods I knew at home. People lacked hope, they were afraid, and they needed to be loved. There were lots of reasons people turned to drugs in these neighborhoods. I ruminated on how these people could be helped. I was of a mind with Pastor Steve—prayer was at the top of my list. In some instances there seemed to be no earthly solution.

I spent the rest of the day in my own prayer and contemplation. Was there some lesson in this for me that I could take back home so I would be able to help this most desperate group of God's people? There were plenty of street addicts I encountered in my workdays on the streets of San Jose, California.

CHAPTER 13

Working as an unknown person in the trenches with the homeless had some real advantages. I was learning firsthand what it was like to be one of those very people I was trying to help in my work with Truck of Love. It was hard to be the one being cared for and being cared about. It was hard to be silent and not offer suggestions of things I thought would work better than what I was currently experiencing. I was definitely having strong feelings about including the patrons in the solution to their own problems (going back to that first kitchen where my offer of help had been so vehemently rejected).

That night I went to the Inner City Shelter where Della steered the overflow Emmaus crowd. After lights out, I sat under the covers of my finally dry sleeping bag. In the darkened room, under the cover with only a flashlight for illumination, I wrote a note to Pastor Steve:

To Whom it May Concern:

Your loving care of us homeless is greatly appreciated. It would be marvelous if you would allow us to return the favor by repaying you by doing small chores. Maybe we could do some chores that are disagree-

*able to your other volunteers. Please give it some thought. Present it
to the powers that be.
Yours very truly,*

A very grateful homeless admirer.

I delivered the note to Emmaus House in the morning and
spent the rest of the day on the bus trying to find new shelters. I
have no idea if the note reached the "powers that be" or if any
action was taken. I did pray that they would think this was a good
idea.

Later that day I found the Salvation Army Armory. I got there
just in time for their 5:00 p.m. check-in time (each shelter was
slightly different). They gave me a voucher for dinner at 6:00 p.m.
at the kitchen across the street.

It was at this kitchen I met a wonderful woman who made
Della look average. This woman obviously had the soul of an
angel and the demeanor of a gentle saint. She was so cheerful and
loving that I felt immediately welcome. She assumed the duty of
making sure everyone had enough to eat. She made sure the other
volunteers took time to sit and talk with the clients of the kitchen.
She was responsible for creating an atmosphere that was welcoming, warm, and homey.

When she came near me I asked, "Is this type of hospitality
typical of the Salvation Army?"

"No," she said. "We're supposed to feed people, then clear
them out for the next group to get fed. But I don't go along with
that philosophy. People need more than food when they eat. They
need fellowship too."

These magic words were more loving than I had hoped to
hear. Now that I heard them, I longed to hear more similar senti-
ments. (I was tired of hearing: "Here, eat. Now when you're finished bus your tray over there.")

The food groups in the soup kitchens and shelters were pretty simple. The small portions were full of carbohydrates and fats —high energy, stick to the ribs food. It certainly stuck to my ribs. No matter how much I walked, I was not losing any weight. Carrying my own large bulk plus a sixty-five pound backpack was getting pretty exhausting!

My time began to be much harder as the days went by. I was experiencing serious sleep deprivation. Sleeping outside, I heard noises all night. Sleeping in shelters I heard noises all night. I never got the deep sleep where I was used to experiencing my dreams. The dreams had guided me here. Now I was unable to experience these gifts of guidance from my God. I was feeling more alone and without direction with each passing day.

I wanted to try again to get into the Potters House. I had learned that it housed the overflow from the Phoenix House that housed men and women infected with the HIV-AIDS virus. This time I was successful and staked out my squares of linoleum. While sleeping in the Potters House I became the food source for what seemed like all the mosquitoes in Savannah. Not knowing a lot about the transmittal of the HIV-AIDS virus, I wondered if I could catch it from a mosquito bite.

Thoughts of illness and the usual sleeping room sounds gave me another restless night's sleep. Upon awakening I met a very tall, very thin man who looked to be in his early twenties. I remembered meeting him on a previous night in another shelter. So I stopped him and said, "Hi, do you remember me?"

"Oh, yeah, I remember you. I'll see you later."

Homeless relationships were really interesting, kind of non-existent, I thought to myself.

I found a shady spot outside on the sidewalk and sat down under a tree. I was writing in my journal and after a time the same young man came by.

"What are you doing?" he said.

I explained I was writing in my journal. He seemed intrigued and introduced himself as Tony. The day was so hot that by this time I was covered in perspiration. My shirt was drenched.

"You look pretty wet," Tony said to me. "Do you want to come with me to my friend's house for a glass of water or something?"

That sounded like a great idea to me and I exclaimed a loud, "Yes! I'd love to!"

We walked a short way before arriving at a house with a front screen door held on by only the bottom hinges. There were empty beer cans lining the front and, as I noticed later, the back entrances to the house. This was definitely a bachelor pad, I thought. But then it dawned on me that this disarray I saw went way beyond the norm of regular guys. There was something wrong here.

Tony knocked on the door and a loud voice from inside barked, "Who is it?"

"It's me, Tony," he said.

A man, five foot ten dressed in cowboy boots and jeans, with long blond hair came to the door. He was very thin and had a tattoo on his right arm—just above the elbow. He squinted like he'd not had a glimpse of daylight in a while. In his hand was a bottle of beer. He bellowed, "WHO THE HELL IS THIS GUY?!"

"He's been in the shelter with me and wants to use the toilet and get a drink of water, Lyle," Tony answered.

Lyle turned without saying a word. The two of us followed behind him through the dark interior where I could see several people I recognized from the shelters. Motioning to me he commanded, "You! Don't take too long in the toilet." And added sarcastically, "The water's in the sink."

I thanked him and went into the disgusting space called a bathroom. When I emerged I could smell marijuana, mixed with another unknown odor that reminded me of burning tires. I didn't ask any questions, but the mystery was soon solved when the man from the door asked if I wanted a hit of crack cocaine.

"NO, thank you!" I said as I bid a hasty retreat out the back door, which also hung by only it's lower hinges.

Tony was behind me calling out his personal advice: "Unless you have money for a woman or crack, Lyle won't let you in. So I wouldn't come back, if I were you." He slammed the door.

"Oh, my God! I was just in a crack house and lived to tell about it!"

As fast as I could, I went back to the nearest shelter, Grace House. I told them about Tony and the house. They were already aware of it.

The person at the desk said, "There is nothing we can do about it. The police have tried and so have the neighbors, but no one seems to be able to get enough evidence to arrest or convict anyone. Thanks for the information."

Thoughts of the house and its occupants haunted me the rest of the day. It was apparent that Lyle's power extended far beyond the house. He was the head of a small time Mafia-type gang. I discovered that Tony and others in this gang went in search of people on the streets who owed Lyle money. Guys who panhandled with signs saying "Will work for food," were forced to give up their earnings—any money they'd been given by passers by. The "payment" collected for Lyle was for crack cocaine the guys had "purchased" on credit. The evil in this whole scheme was overwhelming to me. There was a real social structure on the streets—and it wasn't what I was used to seeing or living.

The heat of the day was oppressive. The perspiration flowed down my head, arms, and legs—my whole body was weeping. As I walked even my feet squished from the puddles inside my shoes. I was getting dizzy from dehydration.

The many days without real sleep—in strange places with strange people—were taking their toll. The experience with Lyle, the crack house and the subsequent information I'd gathered made this time unreal. I couldn't think clearly. I felt confused. It seemed like my only reason for going through each day was to find the next shelter where I could spend another night of restlessness. I was losing the reason I'd originally had for this whole experience—to learn more about serving the poor. I felt aimless, out of sorts, irritable. I didn't like the way everyone seemed to use profanity. Racial slurs, jokes at other people's expense were all around me. I was getting angry with the people surrounding me.

I spent that day walking. I felt the need to get as far away from the crack house as I could. I walked for several hours over the Savannah River into South Carolina. As the sun went down that night I was just coming back over the bridge, back into Georgia. Getting out of town and walking helped me clear my head.

I found a quiet bush and laid out my sleeping bag. That night I dreamed bad dreams. I kept seeing Lyle beating on the poorest of the poor.

Waking at first light, I tried to put my nightmares behind me. I was struck this morning by the fact that time had no meaning to me. Here I was. The sun was rising. I had no place to go and no one who was looking for me. I thought about how different this was from my normal back-home life where every minute was planned. I decided I'd just savor this timelessness for a while. It was really freeing to wake up with the sun and go to bed with the night.

I thought about where I would find breakfast and my morning coffee. I'd been surprised by the ease with which I was able to find food while living on the streets. It seemed as if no one had to go hungry if they were willing to look, ask and—maybe—swallow their pride. I wondered what my hardworking ancestors would say about my life today. They would never have asked for a crumb they couldn't provide by their own hard work. Life is very different for the poor on the streets of our country. I could see that the problems faced by the people on the street were more complex because of mental illness, drugs, and violence. It was one thing for me to help people at home. It was proving to be quite different to be one of the people who are served.

CHAPTER 14

The chiggers (little Southern burrowing bugs) had burrowed into the skin on my neck and legs. I walked and scratched—making my skin raw. Some of my friends of the road had told me to rub mud into the affected areas. I'd done that, but where my skin was fresh, they found new habitats and the itching continued.

With the sweat pouring, the mud running and the constant twitching with itch, I had little time to think about how my joints were becoming stiff from the weight of the backpack and how the sun left a scorched feeling on the top of my bald head. I was quite a sight as I trudged along!

But, today was a new day. The road across the river was calling me North. I love morning and this one was no exception. I found Highway 95 and the tree lined green grass expanse of road. The median was like a California golf course, mowed and manicured. The constant rain created a landscape lush and vibrantly green. It was that constant rain that also caused me to carry plastic bags to cover my belongings at all times.

Hitchhiking that day up Highway 95 I saw signs at each off ramp warning against just what I was doing: hitchhiking. I kept on putting out my sign hoping to get short rides. The trip from

Savannah, Georgia to Raleigh, North Carolina (where I'd decided to go) was less than a five-hour trip by car. I was determined to enjoy every inch of the countryside.

Finally a car pulled up and an old man offered to drive me the next few miles. Being that I was a guest in his car, I was privileged to his wisdom on whatever topic he chose. "If'n yer in a hurry, y'all shod'n be hithik'n in the firs place. I'll tell ya why. Most folks roun here are homebodies an don get out much. Nope, not here ya don. Nope! If ya got relatives who's sick or an anniversy like me n my wife did las week, thin you go and visit. But the scenery don't change none. Everythin ya wants ter see is right here."

I was curious why the old fellow was out on the road—given his little lecture. So I asked.

He replied: "Jes geetin away from the wife fer awhile—and 'sides, I need gas."

After he let me off, I walked til evening. Several times I checked to see if my sign was still attached. It was, but no more rides were offered.

About the time I had decided to get away from the noise of the freeway to set up my meager camp, I saw what looked like a man lying flat on the ground. I hastened over to where he was lying by the road, his backpack still attached. His eyes were shut and he looked like he was in serious distress. I shouted "Hey! Can you hear me?"

One of his eyes fluttered open and he gave a weak nod of his head. He whispered feebly, "Do you have some water you can spare?"

"Sure" I said, "I have lots." Handing him the one bottle I had left I instructed him: "Drink all you can."

I took off my backpack and helped him off with his—hoping that would help cool us both. The late afternoon heat was oppressive.

Passed out

"Can you move?" I asked. "Or would you like me to get something to shade your face?"

Without talking he dragged himself into the shade of a nearby tree.

"How did you get yourself into such a fix?" I asked.

He was perking up from the water and the shade and he said: "I ran out of money in the last town I was in and I decided to try hitchhiking, but no one would pick me up. I've been on the road walking for two days and not even one person has stopped. No one even saw me when I laid down. I tried standing up a while ago, but felt dizzy so laid down again. Then you came along. Thanks!"

I had a little Cliff Bar left and offered it to him. He seemed to get a little better with each bite.

"Are you going to be alright now?" I asked. "I can stay here for a while if you'd like me to."

"I could really use something cool to wipe my face," he said.

I happened to have my emergency "handiwipes" which I offered. We continued to sit and relax together as we cooled off.

Pretty soon he said he felt well enough to travel on. "I'm still a little dizzy, but I'm going to make it alright now. God sent you along at just the right moment!"

Thinking how great it was to hear someone speak words I felt so often, I replied enthusiastically: "You're absolutely right! God does that!"

Getting up and bidding each other good bye, I thought about how not one motorist passing on the road had even slowed down, let alone stopped to see if we needed help. I stored that thought with my growing list of gripes against people who apparently didn't see and didn't care.

The road to Raleigh lasted five days. It was painfully slow and somewhat dangerous. Lots of people passed me. I imagine my large size and lack of cleanliness was a factor in my inability to get a ride. I probably gave off "bad vibes" because I was really tired and very grumpy.

I began to feel like a leper. However, in my optimistic moments, I'd feel like I'd get picked up when the time was right. It seemed the time wasn't right. One day a group of people in a red sedan stopped about 100 yards in front of me. The driver got out next to the car and yelled for me to run. I gathered the last of my waning energy as I ran; thinking I would soon be able to sit in relative comfort and coolness for at least a few miles. When I was about halfway to the car, the driver hopped back into the car, stepped on the gas and sped away. The passengers thrust their hands through the open windows and gave me gestures with less than a full hand of fingers. I could hear their laughter waft back to me as I slumped onto the ground. I really fought letting them see me like this, but I had no choice—I was exhausted! It seemed like high school all over again. I thought they must have the need to feel superior to someone and today it was me.

I passed through lots of towns on the way to Raleigh. Whether I was on the road or in town, I went unnoticed by people. Maybe they saw me, but they did not acknowledge my presence. One day I walked into a park where people all seemed to know one another. It was as though I was invisible. Maybe they were afraid from my appearance that I was going to ask for money. They couldn't have known how lonely I was becoming. I am a pretty social person. I have an easy time talking to people. I'm pretty friendly. I began to crave human interaction. I missed my wife terribly.

One afternoon on the road to Raleigh, I stopped for a rest in a town park. A woman stopped by where I was sitting. She said she needed a dollar for a drink. When I gave her the dollar, she asked if I'd like to come have a drink with her. I declined. Then I watched her go from person to person asking the same questions. Several people asked her if she wanted to just sit down and talk. She did. I kicked myself for not asking that question—it would have helped her and me at the same time. She looked so satisfied sitting and talking on a park bench—she was getting away from her lonely mundane life. Finally a man accepted her invitation to drink and off they went.

I was learning a lot about the life of homeless people. I could see that many were clear and articulate while some were just wasted by drugs and alcohol. Many had huge hearts ready to be shared and seemed to get a sense of fulfillment out of helping other homeless brothers and sisters. And there were those who were just mean.

Sitting in the park that day, I observed lots of people. Thinking how, in my work in California, I often carried an extra bag of fruit and a 12-pack of water to give out to the homeless people, I decided to take my own poll on the park activities. After two hours of observing, I counted 210 regular park goers who had been approached by someone who appeared homeless. Out of those 210 about 72 people had responded to the homeless in some way. One park patron took orders for food and drinks—most of the homeless just wanted something cold to drink.

I approached the man who was taking food orders and said: "You're pretty smart not to give money to these guys. You've done this before? Need some help?"

He smiled and told me he was an undercover policeman. He was a "narc" trying to catch guys selling drugs.

"Are you telling me that you're investigating these guys and buying them food and drinks?" I asked in astonishment.

"Sure" he said. "It's a hot day and people get thirsty, so why not get them something to eat or drink? They're human beings, they have needs. Don't you?"

I loved hearing this from a policeman. But I couldn't quite understand why he had shared the nature of his undercover work with me. "Aren't you afraid that I'll tell these guys who you are and they won't want to have anything to do with you?"

"Now, why would you want to go and do that? Besides they know me. I think I'm pretty safe. Remember, friend, we're all in this together. We need to work as a team. Don't you agree?" said the cop.

I had no argument with that. I especially liked the way he called me "friend." He had no way to know what I did in my other life. To him I was just a guy passing through. He was a man trying to help the guys in his hometown. He continued, "I truly like these guys and I know they need protection."

My discussion with him really bolstered my beaten spirits. He told me about what the police in his town were trying to do with the homeless population. I shared with him my experience with Lyle in the crackhouse. He knew what was going on in the big cities. His response was: "One of these days the guys like Lyle will screw up and we'll be on him like a bee on honey. Believe me, that day is coming."

I felt honored to be taken into his confidence and asked him why he was sharing his information so freely with me. His simple answer was: "Because you asked." He continued on, "I'm here to protect as many of my friends as I can—nothing more, nothing less. We're family here in this town and I'm proud to be a part of it. Christmastime, Thanksgiving, birthdays—they are all important to us. There's nothing better than giving someone a sense of self-worth. I know they'd do the same for me. They know that I'm their friend."

It was late. I hastened that day to find a place to write down my thoughts. I felt encouraged seeing that there were people in this town who helped because they knew the intrinsic worth of a person. It was good to know that this man and maybe others understood that people are good and worthy of our time and energy just by virtue of being human beings, children of God.

CHAPTER 15

Back on the road to Raleigh on High-
way 95 I walked up over a small rise and saw a small diner in the
distance. It looked like a train car. When I reached the gravel parking lot I happened to look at the highway where a grey pickup
truck riding high on huge tires was passing by. Three men in the
seat glared at me. There were four spotlights on the roof of the cab
and a gun in the rack in the rear window. I opened the front door
of the diner as the truck kept on going.

A waitress greeted me. She asked: "Hi there. What'll you have?"

I ordered a cup of coffee and a turkey sandwich and loosened
my backpack so I could place it on the floor.

The waitress returned with my order in a bag. "You know
those guys in the truck?" she asked.

I turned around and could see the same grey truck now parked
in the gravel parking lot in front of the diner. "No," I replied.

"Well, here's your lunch. It's none of my business, but I'd drag
that backpack on the floor and pretend you're gonna use the bathroom. I'll cover for you." She pointed her pencil as though giving
me directions to the bathroom.

I did as she said and she met me at the back door. "What do you think those guys are gonna try?" I asked, thinking I already knew the answer.

"I've seen it plenty of times. The look in their eyes—just sitting and waiting. Those guys are out to hurt someone and you are the one. Just walk through the gully and the ferns out back. You'll find a dirt road about a quarter of a mile down. Oh, yeah, lose the sign on your pack—or put it right."

I gave her a quizzical look. She answered my unspoken questions with, "It's upside down."

I followed her instructions and as I wove through the underbrush away from the diner I heard the words to the old Johnny Horton song: "I ran through the briars and I ran through the brambles and I ran through the bushes where the rabbit couldn't go."

Old Man makes a break
out the back door of the diner.

That night I found a small clearing away from the main high-way. I spread out my sleeping bag (still damp from the rain and humidity) with thoughts of life, liberty and the pursuit of happiness filling my mind. What in the world made men act the way those three were threatening. What happiness do people get by intimidating others? I was very confused.

Sleep overtook me in the safety of the trees off the road.

CHAPTER 16

Waking early in the filtered morning light, I smelled something coming from the near vicinity of my backpack. I went to investigate and get rid of whatever it might be. Unfortunately I caught sight of the salt marks on my t-shirt—under my arms and around the collar and realized the awful odor was me. I wasn't quite sure when or where I was going to be able to bathe. So for the moment I had to ignore myself!

Rolling up my sleeping bag I felt very thankful for life and the wealth of experiences I was having. A near miss with my life, but the wonderful generosity of a woman who wasn't going to allow violence that she could prevent. My bones ached something terrible. I dreaded the inevitable lifting of the backpack onto my shoulders and the miles to go before I could stop that day. "How can I do this one more day and one more night?" I said to myself.

My walk this day was no less eventful. Cars passing by with guys hanging out the windows to yell: "Hey, you LOSER, did someone dump you?" More cat calls, whistles, and "Hey you fat bag of #&*#@, can't you afford a car? You white trash!" There were lots of people willing to exert themselves in order to laugh at my expense.

It was a gloomy, painful time. But I knew I was where God had called me to be. The people sharing their dismal words and gestures didn't know me or who I was. My head throbbed and the pity party took over. I was heartsick with loneliness—even though I knew I was never alone. I knew my God was walking with me. But my loneliness was for the comfort of another human being to share my pain. The loneliness was leading me into a feeling of hopelessness. My spirit was heavy. My body was sick and exhausted.

Thirty six hours of walking on Highway 95 and finally a passing motorist saw my "North" sign. The car stopped just under the sign stating: "Raleigh 38 miles."

I ran to the rider's side door and a woman greeted me with: "Ya got any money?"

I looked in the back seat where two boys sat. They appeared to be about 8 and10 years old.

"Yes," I said. "I have some money."

"Good," she said, "Hop in, I need gas bad."

I did just as I was told. Sitting there in relative comfort I listened as she told me her story. She had fled from her abusive husband who had threatened to kill her and the boys. She was homeless, on her way to her mother's house for a few days. There she would figure out her plan.

The boys invited me to have a bologna sandwich. I hesitated and the mother said, "We've got plenty. Besides when we get to Grandma's house she'll want to fill the car with food before we leave to go wherever we're going."

We stopped for gas before lunch and the mother's instructions to her children were very clear: "Everyone go to the bathroom and wash your hands so you can come back and make the sandwiches."

The boys scurried off to the bathroom, I filled the tank with gas, and the woman opened the hood of the car to check the oil. I bought four extra quarts of oil—just in case she'd have need for them.

The boys came back, we all got into the car and it was time to make sandwiches. The boys were giggling in the back seat. I turned to see what was going on and saw the older boy dissolved in laughter and the younger boy squirming in his seat. He leaned to one side and scrapped what was left of a tomato from the bottom of his pants. In his haste to get going, he'd forgotten they'd left the sandwich tomatoes on the seat! The older boy, seeing my smile, was encouraged to grab a handful of the tomato muck that he promptly threw at his little brother. About this time the mom slammed down the hood of the car and climbed into the driver's seat. The little boy ducked the flying tomato and the mom felt it slap into the back of her head. She angrily screamed: "Don't waste food! What is Grandma going to think when she sees the mess in the car?"

Undaunted the boys continued the fun flinging spoonfuls of mayonnaise at each other. With the mom yelling and the kids laughing it was like a carnival in the old station wagon. By the time we reached the city limits of Raleigh I'd had enough fun to last me for a while. I asked the mom to drop me off.

"But it's another three miles to town," she said. Don't you want to go in a little closer?"

"No, this is just fine," I replied. I was thankful for the ride, but very glad to escape the chaos of the two boys who were on the verge of out-of-control.

The tomato and mayonnaise filled station wagon came to a slow stop by the side of the road and she let me out.

"Thank you so much for the ride," I said. Addressing the boys in the back seat I continued: "And guys, this is the most fun I've had for a long time."

They both smiled and filled their faces with the rest of the bologna sandwiches.

I could see the car lurch from side to side as they drove away. Through the rear window I saw the boys bouncing up and down trying to avoid their mom as she swiped her arm at them from the front seat. Her screaming mantra of "bad boys" escaped from the open windows and faintly reached me as I stood there watching them disappear into the distance.

That small family had made me think of my own childhood, being the youngest of three boys with a single mother. My mother too had a long reach from the front seat and we would feel her swipes in varying degrees of hardness depending on where we sat in the back seat. My childhood had been pretty hard. I hoped that day that these boys would have an easier youth than I'd had.

"Goodbye food fight"

CHAPTER 17

That first evening in Raleigh I pulled out the flashlight my wife, Sue, had given me for the trip. It was dark and I was in an unfamiliar park. I peered into various clumps of bushes finally settling on one that was out of the way of the lights of passing cars. I quickly unrolled my sleeping bag. Before falling asleep, I got out my journal and by the dim light I wrote down the events of the last few days. Then I pulled out a little book I'd brought for purposes of prayer and meditation called "The Imitation of Christ." I fell asleep with the book under my head.

Sometime later I was awakened. The bushes next to me rustled, and an angry voice in the darkness said: "Hey, buddy, this is my spot."

Not wanting to create a problem, I pulled together my belongings, climbed out from under the bush and sat on a nearby bench wondering what to do now. As I looked around the area, I saw the other nearby benches were inhabited by what appeared to be homeless men. One of them sleepily looked up at me in what seemed to be an unfriendly manner. I tried to start a conversation with him, but he was silent. I decided I'd stay here for the night and arranged my belongings within my reach and lay down to sleep.

As soon as dawn broke the three unkempt men inhabiting benches began to stir. I'd not slept much and so I was ready for them with: "Good morning. Mac Donald's is open. Who wants a cup of coffee?" The apparent leader of the three wiped his eyes and nodded saying: "Yeah, sure."

I said: "Do any of you want anything in your coffee?"

"Yeah," said the spokesman. "Get as much of everything as they'll let you take. We'll use it all."

"Do you want to take a walk over and help me with the coffee?" I queried.

"No, they don't let none of us in there any more," he replied.

I returned with some food and extra coffees. The men silently took what I offered. I did get one smile and one nod of thanks, but the third just took the food and drink and began to eat.

I was interested in these three and asked the silent one how he'd met up with the other two.

"Oh," said the designated speaker. "He don't talk."

I let the comment slide. But then he continued, "We only known each other for a couple of months. We met at the shelter downtown. We don't go there no more neither. So, we hang out together."

"Where are you from?" I asked.

"Somewhere in Texas. I can't remember where. I was three when my Mom died. My Dad kicked me and my sister out when she was fifteen. I guess I was about five or six. I don't know exac'ly. My sister tried to git me through school as bes she could, but we did'n have no relatives and we lived on the street kinda like I do now. She earned enough money for us to live, but one day she jes never came back."

When I asked what happened he continued, "I was in the third grade and my teacher said that my sister had been arrested for being a prostitute. She told me that I should go to my relatives after school and they would take care of me. The teacher did'n know that I lived in an abandoned house and that I did'n know no relatives. I went down to the police station and they let me see my sister. She said she'd be there a while, but she'd be out to get me and we'd move somewhere else. I never saw her agin. I bin on my own ever since. I ain't got but a third grade education. But I ain't complainin'. There's lots of odd jobs I taught myself to do."

I asked him: "So, what about your friends?"

"Al and I watch over Seth. Seth don't talk at all. He got real mad at his wife one night three or four years ago and left the house after having a few drinks. When he cooled off he started to go on back to his house. On the way he saw a car wreck—a real blazer. The car was on it's top. The police and ambulances were all over the place. So, Seth stopped and went over to check it out like ev'ryone else's doin'. Turned out it was his wife and two kids burned to death in the car. He only talks about it when he's real drunk. But when he drinks, he tries to kill hisself. So Al and I watch out for him. You know what I mean."

I was overcome with thankfulness that I was there to hear this story. In my wildest imagination I couldn't have guessed the reasons why these three were on the street. They took off and I sat there and cried. It didn't seem to matter where I stayed or even what happened to me. It was raining and I was soon drenched. I stayed wet through that night.

I started to walk. I had no destination. I was lost in Seth's story. Before I knew it darkness was engulfing me and I realized I'd missed any opportunity I might have

He never spoke again!

134

had to find a shelter for that night. My back and hip joints were hurting so badly that I had to find a place to at least sit down. I found a fast food restaurant and ordered some fries and a coffee. I came out of my fog and realized I hadn't eaten since the morning with Seth and his protectors. I had no idea where I would sleep that night.

I left the restaurant and took off walking. I found myself in a downtown area of large office buildings. Behind a large medical complex, I saw a dumpster that was protected by a padlocked chain link fence. I thought this looked like a safe place to hide for the night. I might even get an uninterrupted night's sleep. The dumpster backed up to a loading dock. I climbed up on the dock and carefully lowered myself to the ground behind the dumpster. In the relative privacy, I unloaded my backpack and sleeping bag. I wearily crawled into my damp sleeping bag and was asleep almost before my head was fully at rest.

I leapt to my feet still inside the sleeping bag at about 3:30 a.m. In the black darkness, I had been awakened by the sound of the lock being opened on the chain that held the gate to my sanctuary closed. I could hear the whine of the forks on a garbage truck being lowered toward the dumpster and I made one huge jump for the loading dock. Up went the dumpster and down it crashed —right where I'd been sleeping just moments before!

My heart was racing and my ears were ringing so I could barely hear what the garbage man yelled at me as he closed and locked the gate. It was something about being stupid and dangerous with lots of bad words in between. I realized he was as frightened and surprised as I was. I yelled an apology at him as I gathered my belongings to look for another spot to finish my night. I was wide-awake.

At morning light my thoughts were all about finding a place for that night's safe sleep.

CHAPTER 18

The city transit system of Raleigh was good. It was now easy to find anything I was looking for. After some recommendations from fellow "travelers," I found the Saint Vincent de Paul shelter. The volunteers were helpful and kind and served me and the other homeless men efficiently and well. But I once again had the feeling I'd had in Savannah. The volunteers did their job so well that there was no need or any opportunity for the homeless people to help out. We were there simply for a hand-out. The food was good, but again I felt useless—almost as if I wasn't human. It was good to have a safe, clean place to sleep. But I felt like an object of these people's good deeds.

The next day I decided to try an experiment. I thought I'd go to one of the other shelters in town and offer myself as a volunteer. I thought that way I could be accepted as a "real person" and get to eat.

I spent the day trying to find a place to clean up. There were some gas stations that had restrooms that could be opened by inserting quarters. I shaved and cleaned my body as best I could. I changed into my black pants and white shirt and found a shelter just before dinner time. I walked into the kitchen and offered my services. They put me to work cutting vegetables.

Sure enough after serving the homeless people who came through the line, we kitchen volunteers got to eat. I was now enjoying both worlds!

After clean up with the other members of the kitchen crew, I wrote an anonymous note for the person in charge. I told her what I'd done and how good it made me feel. I made sure to emphasize what I thought was important. "...we homeless people are looking for the same pride in what we do as you, the volunteers...is there any way we can work together in the future?" This experience reminded me once again of how I wanted to be respected for who I am. It seemed like when the volunteers did their work in isolation, they were not really getting to know anything about the people they served. I was getting tired of being invisible.

The next day as I walked around town, I saw a sign in the window of a Dry cleaning shop. It said: "help wanted" in both English and Chinese figures. Next to the sign inside the window, on a stool, sat a small old hunched over man. He stared out the window at the people passing by—like a cat with thinning white hair. I decided to take a chance and ask about the job.

I entered the shop and approached the lady behind the counter. She was Asian, in her forties and just stared at me. I greeted her and asked about the job. She asked if I'd worked in a dry cleaner before. I had not.

"What do you expect to be paid?"

"I'll leave that up to you."

She put me to work. I worked all day. It was hot and the air was filled with the cleaning fluid fumes. My eyes burned and my throat hurt. I sorted, loaded, folded, bagged, tagged, and hung up the cleaned clothes. Hour after hour I sweated through the day. After six hours of this I was ready to leave. I stopped to get my pay —she handed me ten dollars! That was the last job I took.

CHAPTER 19

I noticed in my travels that there were very few young people hanging out with the older folks. The teens I did see hung out in groups of other teens. They appeared to help each other. It felt to me like the older you were on the street the more alone you were.

I was feeling sick and my joints were aching from sleeping on hard surfaces and from the long days of walking with the heavy backpack. I was having difficulty staying in the shelters. The shelters were beehives of constant snoring and rustling. Even though smoking wasn't allowed in the shelters, people seemed to drag the smoke inside with them from their outdoor smoking dens. It was the smoke that bothered me the most, causing my eyes to burn and ooze yellow sticky goo. Sleeping outdoors soon became more desirable to me than the safety of the shelter.

That night sleeping outdoors became a necessity, because when I went to check in to the shelter, the woman at the front desk turned me away. "You can't stay here," she said. "You have an eye infection. We can't have anyone else getting sick because of you. Sorry."

But my sleeping bag was still quite wet from the constant rain. I decided I'd lay out the sleeping bag to see if it would dry. I meandered back to the same park where I'd been so unceremoniously rejected from the bush in the middle of that first night in Raleigh. I was just unrolling the bag to lay it across the bench where I'd slept when a man walked up to me and simply said, "I'm Jay."

After some small talk, Jay offered to treat me to a meal from his favorite Chinese restaurant. I discovered that if Jay couldn't get into a shelter or find a place for an evening meal he would opt for Chinese food. He loved Chinese food. He said, "Come on!"

And I went. The Chinese restaurant was not too far away and once we got there we walked around to the back of the building. Jay excitedly told me this was the best Chinese food in the city. Then he opened the top of the dumpster and climbed in.

I couldn't believe what I was doing! "My God," I thought. "What have I become?" I wanted to hide. I didn't want anyone to see me. I felt like I'd become a leper.

Jay encouraged me. "If you're gonna survive on the street you have to learn how to dumpster dive."

Dumpster dive, I thought! But I was hungry and they weren't going to let me into the shelter.

Jay added: "Look at it this way, Old Man. If you don't like the kind of food you get out of a dumpster, you don't have to eat it. If you like it then you're gonna live to see another day."

Jay

Jay and Old Man dining out

The restaurant workers had just dumped a new batch of left-overs, some in containers. Jay knew just where to look. It was now dark and he went to work. He poked around, all the time giving me advice on how to find the best of what was there. I began to be intrigued by what he was doing. But I looked on in disbelief as I contemplated getting in there myself. The smell of soured food in combination with the newer offerings was sickening in itself. I was already sick. What would this do to me?

I knew if the occasion arose, that I had committed myself to this part of the adventure. But I was horrified that the time had come.

I compromised by complimenting Jay on his ability to find what was best. He knew how to find only the choicest, warm containers of half eaten food. He'd use his flashlight and his nose to test for quality of appearance and smell. One by one he carefully chose boxes and handed them out to me. I made sure nothing got lost. Once he was satisfied that he'd gotten enough food for us from the stinky dining hall, he jumped out of the filthy box and slammed the rusty lid shut!

Carrying our precious cargo, we returned to the park and washed our hands in the huge white fountain there. I was hungry and began to anticipate with some joy my impending gourmet meal.

It was better than either of us had imagined! Fried shrimp, egg fried rice and chow mein were my immediate favorites. Then we went on to plain noodles and rice with some Peking duck and vegetables. We ate it all! We were stuffed and it felt good to have a full stomach. We topped it off with a long drink of water from the drinking fountain.

As we dined, Jay explained the facts to me. He said whenever he dumpster dived, he tried to leave the area on the ground around the dumpster cleaner than when he had arrived. Fact number two caught me off guard when he said that the police arrested anyone they saw in a dumpster. Jay felt that was because of the insurance companies that feared "divers" like us would get hurt in the dumpster or sick from the food and sue the restaurants that used them.

I queried, "Do you mean that we could be jailed for what we were doing?"

"Yup," he said. "But no one ever pays us no mind."

Exhaustion overcame both of us. It was very late. We crawled into a darkened cave of branches by the wall of the park. It was a secluded space that many homeless people used.

I tried to get comfortable enough to sleep, but began to feel even more sick. My stomach felt like it was going to explode! As my body got hotter and hotter I curled up into a fetal position. Jay snored by my side.

I thought, "It couldn't be the food. Jay doesn't seem to be bothered. We ate the same thing."

Jay snored while I prayed. "Lord, if this is the way I'm going to die, I go willingly. If my mission is not over, than I pray 'thank you.' Thank you for the lesson I am going to learn from this experience of my body not being healthy and my mind being so very tired. Thank you, Lord!"

I could not get comfortable. I turned from one side to the other. In my mind I went over the whole food procedure. Jay had instructed me to wash my hands before I ate. We had used every precaution to keep the food clean.

When I couldn't stand it any more and I knew the inevitable was about to happen, I crawled a short way away from my sleeping bag and I started to vomit. All the food I'd eaten came up. Over and over I pleaded with God to let me sleep. My eyes burned and my head pounded. There was a rhythm to the pain. I prayed for sleep, but the hammer and anvil resounded in my skull. My wakefulness became confused. I wondered where I was, why I was here, what I'd said "yes" to. Then I'd realize I'd said "yes" to God's call. But I hadn't said "yes" to this.

As I huddled under the bush, my thoughts swirled from the people I'd met on the street to my family back home. I'd encountered love and hate in both extremes. At one moment I'd cry with pain and sadness, another moment I'd laugh at some fun memory. Mostly I gave in to tears that washed my burning eyes but brought no relief from the stinging feeling and blurred vision. I was miserable!

Light came and then again darkness. More than a day had passed. Jay came in and out of my awareness. My joints ached. Turning from side to side took almost more strength than I possessed. The dreams through half-wakefulness continued. I was alone. There was no place to go to get relief. I kept up the praying. God was my only hope!

I felt like a real social outcast—shunned by all and wanted by none. My eyes showed me only shadowy outlines. I couldn't see. What was I going to do? I felt the evilness of my situation engulf me. I had no protection from it. Jay kept coming back—he'd bring water and ask if I was okay. I knew he was there, but I couldn't interact with anyone.

When the light of morning dawned at last, it hurt my eyes. Even through closed eyelids, the brightness of the day burned me. I felt the need to write in my journal all I had been feeling, but I couldn't see the page. I used my finger as a guide and scribbled my thoughts all over the paper. I needed to write this down. I could see only the glow of people or objects passing by my bush. The page I was writing on had some smudges that I thought might be my last thoughts put to paper. I just let my hand write til the edge of the page and then I'd go back to the left side —avoiding the smudges I thought might be previous scribblings.

The deafening sounds of skateboarders woke Jay, who was asleep near me. I heard his voice but could not see his face. He said, "Those guys on skateboards—we don't mix too well. They're kids—homeless like us. But they're always looking to take something from me. Some of them have clubs and threaten us guys in the park. If you're in their way, they'll take your money and food and steal ya' blind. It's best to avoid them if you can. Ya' know what I mean?"

I had stopped writing—I was listening to Jay. Now he got up and left me alone in the bushes. I felt somewhat abandoned, but did not share his fear of the teens.

Several hours later, Jay returned. He had brought some food. I could smell it, but not being able to see, I wondered out loud, "Did you get this from a dumpster?"

"No," he said. "I found a wallet in the park. I saw a family walking away from the area and asked the Dad if he had lost a wallet. The man was so glad to get the wallet that he gave me ten dollars. So, here's the food."

I was really happy to hear Jay had been so honest, but I couldn't resist asking, "How come you didn't just keep the wallet?"

"Cause, I saw the guy who lost it," came his simple, beautiful reply. He went on. "If I'd lost my stuff I'd want them to give it back. Wouldn't you?"

"I sure would, Jay. You're a man after my own heart. I'm glad you gave the wallet back."

"Yeah," said Jay. "Me too. And I got ten bucks out of it."

Jay was a quiet, stoic fellow who came and went as he pleased. As we sat there in the bush he began to pack his belongings into a plastic bag he used as his suitcase. He was leaving the home he had so willingly shared with me through these long dark days and nights.

I asked, "Am I going to see you again?"

"It's not good to stay in one spot for too long—if you catch my drift," was all he had to say.

Then he was gone from our bush and from my life.

He left the food. One small bite at a time, I attempted to take in some nourishment. I felt so awful that it was hard to eat anything, but I knew I had to try.

I wanted the sick to end and I prayed for the pain in my joints and my weakness to leave me. I felt terrible. My vision was getting worse. Everything was blurred. It was harder and harder to write in my diary. What I wrote was becoming very confused because I couldn't see the lines on the page. At the least, I tried to write my feelings. I knew if or when I looked back on these days, I would want to remember the intensity of what I was feeling.

I wanted to be indoors for the night. Shakily I hoisted my backpack and emerged from the bush. Exhausted by illness, I trudged through the streets to the nearest homeless shelter. I craved the idea of lying down on a mat that was softer than the ground. Now that Jay was gone, I desired the company of other human beings.

Arriving at the door of the shelter, a woman looked me over before she greeted me with: "Oh, sweetie, the infirmary isn't open today. You can't stay here tonight, you're way too sick. You're liable to infect everyone else."

I was dumbfounded. I didn't know what to do. I'd used an awful lot of energy just getting to this place.

"Where can I go then?" I asked.

"Well you can go to the County General Hospital and have your eyes looked at. But it's not a good idea to infect everyone here with whatever you've got."

"How far is County General?"

"About twelve miles that way," she pointed.

"How can I get there?"

"Maybe there's a kind-hearted soul here who can give you a ride," she offered.

In my delirium, I remembered that Sue had told me to be sure to bring my Kaiser insurance card with me. I surprised her with my next question: "Is there a Kaiser hospital nearby?"

Visibly bewildered, she replied, "Yes, there's a Kaiser about ten blocks down this road. But why do you want to know about Kaiser? County General is the only hospital that will treat you!"

I thanked her for the information and took off at a very slow walk. Her directions weren't very accurate, so after asking several people for new directions, I finally arrived at the Kaiser—it seemed like I'd gone several miles.

Hours of sitting in the Kaiser waiting room rewarded me with a short visit to a doctor who told me I had a severe case of conjunctivitis (pink eye). He gave me drops and told me to get plenty of rest and stay out of the direct sun—as that would make my eyes hurt even more.

Exiting the Kaiser building, I slowly and methodically put one foot in front of the other and made my way back to the bush I'd shared with Jay the past several days. I collapsed under the branches to take a well-deserved nap.

How did homeless people survive? I wondered to myself. This was harsh. No one wanted to be near me. The doctor at Kaiser was happy to "fix" me and get rid of me. I supposed I was on the mend, but what about the other people living on these streets? What did they do when they got sick? I did not like this.

Waking from a fitful sleep. I mustered up enough courage to emerge from my bush and go across the street to the corner store and buy some cheap sunglasses to protect my very tender eyes. Immediately upon wearing the sunglasses, my vision improved. The shadows now had a little more definition.

I went back to the bush thinking about Jay's advice not to stay too long in one place. I rolled up my sleeping bag and stuffed everything into my pack and started my move out of Raleigh and on to new territory. I thought I'd head North to Washington DC. I thought there was a Catholic Worker there—maybe I could work there for a week or so.

CHAPTER 20

Making my way out of Raleigh became a difficult task. Within a few hours and with the help of a few kind-hearted men, I found my way to Interstate 95. With my "north" sign hanging off my back, I struggled to walk. My pack seemed heavier than it had been. I guessed it was because I wasn't feeling quite up to par. The rains came and went and my pack continued to get heavier. I trudged on with my head down against the rain.

I had walked about an hour when a Highway Patrol car stopped right in front of me. The red and blue lights on the car began to flash.

As I neared the car, I could see the face of the patrolman inside. His demeanor was one of exasperation. I wondered if he was as weary as I. Thinking I must be quite a sight, I wondered if he could see my red swollen eyes behind my cheap sunglasses. Apparently he could. Our conversation went like this.

"Hi," I said in my usual friendly way.

"ID (ah deh), please," he stated in a drawl.

I produced my license from my back pocket.

"So, you're from California?" he asked.

"Yes," I said.

"Did you know it's against the law to hitchhike on the Interstate?"

I feigned ignorance, but was as guilty as sin!

"Well, Clahv (the name on my license is 'Clive')…what kind of a name is that?" he continued without pause, "I'm not going to write you a ticket, because you'll probably never pay it. I'm not going to take you to jail because that costs taxpayers money. But I am gonna give you a ride near to where I live."

Thinking a rest in the clink might have felt pretty good, I gave him the expected, "Thank you." But I knew his gesture was not one of politeness.

Before I could get into the patrol car, he told me to empty my backpack onto the wet ground. He was looking for drugs or drug paraphernalia. He seemed visibly angered that he found nothing suspicious in my pile of dirty stinky clothing.

He got onto the car radio to inform the dispatcher that he was heading home for the night—to Fayetteville, North Carolina with a vagrant passenger. He had seen my sign declaring "north." He knew the direction I was attempting to go.

I struggled into the back seat of the patrol car and began to redistribute the mess in my backpack. He turned the car around and began to head directly south. In just ten minutes we were driving through the eastern edge of Raleigh and heading south. Not a word was exchanged between us during the ride. An hour later he pulled into a gas station at the side of the road in Fayetteville, opened the back door and silently ushered me out.

As he pulled out, I found the pay phone. The call I placed was to the Catholic Worker House in Washington DC. A young male voice answered the phone. When I asked about working with them for a week, he informed me that all the residents of the house were on retreat for the next week. He had no authority to tell me to come work there. Although he treated me politely, I felt feelings of contempt for his "no authority" comment. Maybe it was my unspoken anger at the patrolman who had used his authority in such a negative way (I thought).

I felt haggard and dirty because of my days in the bush. I knew I probably smelled somewhat like a rhinoceros. I walked away from the phone and into the gas station. I bought a candy bar (thus I was a customer) and asked the clerk for the key to the bathroom. He reluctantly gave me the key.

I took full advantage of the private space and running water. It felt so good to clean up a little. Then I saw the handwritten sign that hung next to the paper towel dispenser. It stated in bold print: "We have no use here for niggers, bums, or hitchhikers." I was stunned. I began to cry, thinking of all the wonderful people I'd met on my journey—the bums, the niggers, the hitchhikers. I hurt for myself and for all those great people.

I thought, "I have no business here. What am I doing in this place, why has God sent me here?" It was then I made a decision about my next course of action.

I walked back to the clerk and handed him the bathroom key. I thanked him for the use of the restroom. I went outside.

I reached into my pocket and found a quarter. With a "Quo vadis"(which road) prayer, I tossed the coin. I figured "heads" I'd try to go north—"tails" I'd go west and head for home. The coin landed in the dust and I wearily stared at it, stunned. It had landed "tails."

I was too exhausted to comprehend what I'd just decided. Finally after 45 days on the road, I was going home! Blessed home, where I was loved and accepted. Immediately I reached into my backpack and pulled out the "west" sign! Just in case I was being watched, I made a break for a road leading to 401 West. I avoided the main highway feeling I was better safe than sorry.

A sick and tired 'Old Man'

PART
III

CHAPTER 21

I began a new journey. I walked the back roads with sweat pouring down my neck into my shirt under my backpack. Most roads were paved, but many were just wide flat long stretches of hard dirt. Flanked by green fields and trees, these roads were extraordinary! Sometimes I'd take off my shoes so I could feel the dirt against my feet.

On the asphalt roads it felt better to wear my shoes. But my shoes were wearing very thin on the bottom and the heat of the road made the balls of my feet very hot.

Since I was avoiding the main roads I missed lots of possible rides. But at this stage of my journey, I had been burned badly enough that I was more concerned about saving my life. Human contact was something I wanted to avoid right now. So I slowly trudged along the deserted stretches of spectacular countryside. I enjoyed the quiet peacefulness walking along the river. I could feel a tickling of life creeping back into my exhausted body and mind.

As I walked, I daydreamed. Thoughts of my childhood crept in. Life had been so much simpler. The name "Tius" kept coming into my mind. Little by little an old woman's black leathery face came into the focus of my memory.

When I was a small child of about four, I visited my grandmother Franklin to help her with weekend chores. Tius would be there—sitting in the rocking chair on the porch—going back and forth, back and forth. The rickety chair seemed even older than she was. I was young and little, she was big and round and safe. She lived in an old broken down shed behind grandma's house. My grandma referred to it as an "apartment." Whenever I'd be at grandma's house, I'd eventually find my way to the "apartment."

Tius liked to tell stories about her childhood in Louisiana. The details are gone from me, but I remember the warm feeling of listening to her. She told me her mother was a slave. I had no idea what that meant.

Tius had deep lines in her face and when she smiled her lips raised her cheeks—just like parting brown curtains. She was the essence of peace and calm. She and I would sit in front of her apartment. She would rock and I would wait for more stories.

One Sunday, I asked Tius, "Are you a nigger? My Grandma says you are."

To this day I can hear Tius' reply, "Chile', God say what we are. Some says I's a nigger, but they don't know."

Tius taught me all the lessons that I later heard from the Reverend at church. She'd say, "We're all brothers and sisters. We fight with each other because that's what brothers and sisters do. We're always supposed to make up, though. Tha's the hard part."

Another Sunday, after church, Tius asked me to ask Grandma if she could borrow a cup of sugar. She wanted to make lemonade. She told me to ask Grandma and Grandpa if they would like a glass of lemonade. They told me they were too busy, but they didn't look very busy to me. The lemonade was a little sour, but I loved drinking it with Tius.

As I went back into the house through the back porch, Grandma stopped me. "Don't you never ask me for sugar to take to that old

nigger's house again!" She barked, "Young man, we're diff'rent from
Tius. You can't go back over there to play no more!"

The word "nigger" stuck with me. But more than the word, was the
feeling I got as Grandma said it. I also didn't know what to do when I
heard I couldn't visit with Tius. My four-year-old heart was broken.

Soon after that, Tius didn't live in the "apartment" any more. All
Grandpa said was, "You know how your Grandma can be when she gets
something in her head." I never saw Tius again.

The walk along the river had done me a lot of good. I'd
needed the time to think—to clear my head of the hatefulness I'd
experienced. Thinking about Tius was no accident. She'd spent
her life being treated with disdain. I recommitted myself to try to
take whatever God had in store for me, to try to remember to treat
all people with love and respect.

I couldn't remember if it was Saturday or Sunday—the days all
mixed together. But I felt the need to go to church—to be physically in the church building—to receive communion.

I passed through so many small towns. I walked into such
beautiful countryside. Most of it was still a blur, but I could see the
colors. The swelling in my eyes seemed to be lessened, but I still
saw bright halos around everything. Street signs and other signs
were a complete mystery. People's faces were a blur. My sunglasses helped to hide my red eyes from others, but didn't really
help me to see. If I wanted to read a sign, I had to stand directly
in front of it and read letter by letter—moving my head with the
light and shadows helped me decipher the shapes. I passed
through towns named Langton and Liberty. Places that I'd love to
return to some day. Maybe Sue and I could return for a different
kind of adventure.

Because of my health, my state of constant exhaustion, and
my vision problems, I was having a very difficult time finding the
road west. Eventually I came upon Hwy 40 and a truck stop with

lots and lots of trucks. Surely, I thought, there ought to be one driver here who would have enough compassion to give me a ride.

Before I could start my inquiries, the rain cloud that had been following me for some time, let loose. I ran for the nearest bush so I could have time to cover my backpack with plastic. I knew I didn't have the strength to carry a soaked backpack with all that extra water weight.

The energy I'd felt upon seeing all the trucks quickly dissipated as I struggled to cover my backpack. I could barely stand up I was so exhausted. I rested under the bush for a while trying to gain some strength.

Eventually I made my way into the truck stop and headed for the rest room. The place was teeming with action. I'd seen the man in line in front of me drive in one of the long liners. I knew he'd parked it just outside. "Hi," I said. "Where are we?"

He turned toward my voice and could easily see I was having trouble with my vision. He replied, "You're in a truck stop just south of Greensborough, North Carolina. Where are you headed?"

The sound of his happy voice was music to my ears.

"Hey!" he said. "Are you okay? You look like you need a doctor."

I guess I wasn't aware I looked that bad. "I'm gonna be okay now. I saw a doctor in Raleigh."

"Raleigh?" the man repeated. "That's eighty miles away! Have you been walking all that way?"

"Yeah," I replied. "I was picked up by a policeman on Highway 95 when I was hitchhiking. So I've been using the back roads trying to stay out of harm's way. How would you like a rider?"

"It's against the law to hitch rides here in these truck stops," he said. "But I could use some company."

I could hardly contain my excitement. We walked out to his truck, a 45-foot flatbed piled high with bales of wire wrapped hay.

I waited as he unlocked the door. When I climbed into the cab, I asked, "What's your name?"

"I'm on my way to Knoxville, Tennessee. You can call me, 'Tornado,' that's my handle anyway. What's yours?"

"Oh, people just call me 'Old Man'."

That seemed to satisfy him and we both settled into our seats. I was thrilled to be going to Knoxville—that was two hundred and fifty miles!

Curious, I asked, "How'd you get your name?"

"I was on my way to Claremore, Oklahoma during a tornado watch—except I didn't know it was a tornado watch. There wasn't anyone else on the road. I saw a few trucks stopped hunkered down off the side of the road. I noticed there were no animals roaming around—I didn't even see any birds around. I thought it was strange, but I kept on driving. The clouds started to circle and a funnel cloud formed in the pasture off to the left of me. The wind was hitting the truck really hard, but it would come and go. I really didn't figure out what it all meant.

Finally it hit me what was happening! I stepped on the gas thinking I needed to get out of the way—and fast! I didn't want to get stuck in the middle of it. I'd seen the result of twisters and it wasn't a pretty sight. I thought I was safe when the funnel evaporated back into the clouds and the wind began to shift away from me. Right then two more funnels began to form and aimed right at me. They both hit at about the same time. My trailer and all the livestock I was carrying went flying. I watched as the trailer appeared in front of me turning end over end. It could have been a paper plate the way it flew!

I guess I was in shock. The next thing I recall I was with a Highway Patrol officer. He was inviting me to sit in his Patrol car. I couldn't remember anything but a big bump. But I could see some skid marks on the road about fifty feet from where my cab was sitting. The cop began to talk with me. He thought I must have shifted to low to try to stop the truck, but I don't remember.

I do know that I had been heading toward Claremore and when I saw the cop, my cab was turned around in the other direction. My trailer and livestock was scattered all over a ripped up wheat field. All my animals was dead or so bad hurt, that I had to shoot them.

I remember hearing the voice of some other trucker sayin' he'd seen the whole thing and I must be one of the luckiest sons of bitches that had ever lived. He kept sayin the word 'tornado' and I felt as though he was talking 'bout me. From that time on every time someone mentioned the word tornado, I responded 'yeah' or 'whad'ya want?' I've called myself Tornado ever since. That was six years ago."

I enjoyed riding with Tornado for a while. He had lots of stories. He was a little hard to understand because his stories kind of rambled. But, it was his comments about the Vietnam War that stopped me from talking. He told me he'd fought in Vietnam. Then he offered his personal views: "We should've gone and killed every damn one of those bastards. Ain't one of them deserved to live anyhow."

About that time, I felt the need to change the subject. He obviously had an opinion about the war that I didn't share. I resorted to the time-honored "kid" question that used to get me into lots of trouble with my mother: "How much longer til we get there?"

"Not much, maybe an hour er so."

He began to ask me questions like "You ever been in these parts before?" and "What does it mean when someone says 'I knew him when'? Does it mean that you knew someone when they were young or when no one else knew them?" Then a non-truck related noise would occur and he'd mumble, "Sounds like I hit a critter."

He seemed like a pretty lonely fellow.

We drove through patches of heavy rain. Every time the rain would end, Tornado would roll down the window and have a smoke. He commented, "You don't smoke, do you Old Man?"

"Well I used to smoke a lot, but it got too expensive," I replied. Then asked a question of my own, "Does your family live nearby? Where do you call home?"

"I used to live here in Knoxville, but one day I wanted a change of scenery and I packed up my stuff and left."

"What about kids? You have any?" I continued.

"Nope, never wanted kids. I'm just a travlin' man with an itchy heel. What about you Old Man? Why you call yerself Old Man?"

I thought for a minute and then finally said, "I really don't like my real name. Ever since I turned fifty, I looked kind of old. People I work with called me Old Man and it kind of stuck."

Whenever people started asking me personal questions I tried to steer the subject back to them. "What about you? Do you have any family?"

Tornado replied, "I had a brother in Jasper, Missouri, but he died. He was the only one left since my dad died in 1992. I got lots of friends, though and I love listening to my CB (radio)."

Tornado pulled off the road at a truck stop. We both got out and he bid me goodbye saying, "You'll have a better chance of getting a ride from here than from the next stop. Even though it's against the law to hitch a ride in these places, it'll be easier here than on the side of the road. I don't usually pick up hitchhikers, but it's been kind fun tonight. You're a regular nice guy."

I was touched by his friendly farewell. "Yeah," I said as we shook hands, "I'm glad we met too. Maybe we'll cross paths again somewhere down the road."

"Ya never know," he answered as he opened the driver's door, swung his left leg onto the platform and hopped into the big rig and pulled slowly away from where I stood.

A ride in the rain

CHAPTER 22

The darkness and light rain were somehow comforting and I felt grateful to be alive. I did just as Tornado had advised and stayed close to the truck stop hoping it wouldn't be too difficult to get the next ride. I began to get a little chilled from the rain and decided to find shelter in a nearby thicket of what looked to be trees. I huddled on the ground with the trees dripping on me. I'd sleep for a few moments and then wake up—startled and confused. My sickness was befuddling my brain once again and in the next moment I'd decided to myself that I was going to walk into Knoxville to find shelter for the night!

I stiffly got to my feet and hoisted the backpack once again. I walked in the rain for about forty- five minutes with the backpack getting heavier and heavier. It was a huge effort to move one foot in front of the other—the weight of the pack was pulling me down. I couldn't recall another time in my life when I'd felt so exhausted.

I was in town at this point and I came to a bench where I collapsed into a heap on top of my saturated backpack. I couldn't think about what I needed or what to do. In my fatigue I began to pray: "Thank you God for the rain and the pain in my feet and my head. Thanks for home and for another day closer to my love."

The prayer seemed to revive me for another push forward. I walked another mile or so and stopped again. This time I pulled out my drawings and journal pages that were soaked through. I wished I'd put them in a plastic bag like I'd thought about some time ago. I stuffed them back into my pack.

Somehow the idea of shelter for the night made me get up and walk. I came to a street sign that I could make out—it said "Western Street." I read it out loud with a kind of reverence as though it was a promise that I would get to my home in the west. For some unknown reason I thought this street would help me find shelter—so I headed down Western Street. My throbbing feet were burning badly from chafing in my very thin shoes after mile upon mile of walking. My head was confused and I was getting hot now that the rain had let up some.

I thought to myself, "There's got to be some place to stay here." I didn't have much money, but I'd be able to pay something if I had to. (I still had some cash from my truck driving days.)

Suddenly there was a brightly lit sign in a doorway in front of me. Getting close to it I could make out that it was the name of the hotel that occupied the building I was in front of. I'll call it the "No-Tell Motel" to protect the management's reputation.

It was the kind of place that required no ID—just cash in advance and a $10.00 key deposit. I could barely focus on the process of paying. I was issued a key and found my way to my room. The space was private and had a bed. I literally collapsed and was finally able to follow the directions of the doctor in Raleigh—"Get some rest."

I slept for what seemed like a very long time. Sometimes I'd hear sirens and other very loud sounds, but they would only disturb me slightly. I'd be unconscious again before my brain could really register I'd even been disturbed.

When I awoke and actually became conscious of being alive, I got into the shower and let the warm water wash over my whole body. I was in the shower so long that I began to feel guilty for all the homeless people I knew who wouldn't have a shower on this day. Guilty or not though, I enjoyed the heck out of this experience! It felt like I was being baptized and reborn while standing in the Jordan River. I nearly feel asleep on my feet in the water!

Getting out, I dried off. The mirror was completely steamed up so I could not even see the outline of my face. I was sure I wasn't a very pretty picture. But I felt a glow of warmth inside me. I knew God was by my side.

I stayed several nights. It was a pretty cheap place to stay. I slept and slept. It's what I needed.

Once the complete exhaustion had passed, a feeling of emptiness came over me. One night lying awake in the darkened motel room, I felt desperate and overwhelmingly alone. Somewhere in the depths of my being I realized this must be the result of the days and weeks of homelessness. It was taking a toll on my mind and spirit.

I thought back about the people I'd met on this quest. I'd encountered powerless people who had been beaten down by homelessness. I'd seen the intolerance of others who preyed upon the homeless population. I had also witnessed the resilience of some of the homeless people as they made each day an adventure. Over all this I kept coming back to the thoughts of "What am I going to do with all this experience?"

Finally I picked up my pencil and began to write. I thought that if I wrote down my feelings maybe I'd find some solutions or at least some relief from my feelings of desperation.

Writing had just the opposite effect. Feelings of sickness and sadness overcame me. I dropped my pencil and in the privacy of my small room, I cried. I wept uncontrollably. From the depths of my being the cries erupted. I felt useless in my attempts to understand homeless people.

The crying lasted a long time—much too long for my liking (Crying is not something I willingly engage in). When the tears were done I could feel my face was pinched and puckered. My eyes stung and all the muscles in my face hurt. Why had I been given this calling to live among the poor and not be able to understand it or follow through with it in some meaningful way?

I remembered the days of my own youth that were lived in pretty extreme poverty. After the death of my father, my mother had struggled to keep my brothers and me together as a family. Days lived in poverty then were days of togetherness with my brothers. We were like the Three Musketeers: "All for one and one for all!" We'd had lots of fun. Poverty wasn't the first thing on our minds. We were busy about living.

"Thank you, God," I prayed. God's timing was, once again, amazing! If I'd had these thoughts of hopelessness earlier, I'd probably have headed for home even faster. But now that I was somewhat rested, I could put some perspective into my rambling feelings. I now began to laugh. I laughed and laughed! I laughed until I cried.

My pencil seemed to have a mind of it's own. My vision was slightly improved and I could see the page. I wrote about my feelings. Then my pen wrote "God."

God is the common underlying thread in all of us. Each of us has a different story. We are meant to share this story with those we meet. Each of us has our own perspective on life. Each of us is called to live out our lives in some special way. This is what we have to share with others. These ideas, though I had known them before, now took on new meaning. I'd been "hammered on the anvil of God"!

The light was beginning to peek through my present darkness. It was giving me new strength. When I'd begun my journey, I'd really been in the dark. I hadn't had a clue how much strength and endurance it would take to live on the streets of the United States. I'd worked with poor people for a long time, but I didn't know anything about their daily struggles. I was beginning to see. I was learning. I realized that God had been hearing my pleas all along. His answers were what I needed, not what I thought I wanted.

I looked around my simple room. It seemed to have a permanent haze from all the smokers who'd lived there before me. The bathroom caught my eye. It wasn't fancy, but there it was—it was available whenever I wanted to use it. Here in the room I had privacy and I was not in danger of being arrested. I was safe! What a gift.

I thought more about the people I'd been meeting on the streets. I was a great observer of behavior and I recalled how the street people brightened up any time a person noticed them. When a person would stop and speak to a homeless person, that person would stand up straighter, and seem to have a clarity that might not have existed before. It was amazing how little it took for a person not to feel alone. A smile, a nod of the head, even a glance of recognition could bring a glimmer of new life.

The people I had been meeting on the street valued someone listening to them. I noticed that some of the fights that broke out were as a result of one person not listening to another. Constant drug use made it difficult for people to listen to each other—so in some places violence was a frequent occurrence. The reverse seemed also to be true. When people listened to each other then the physical gestures were of friendship—slapping on the back, glad-handing in a gesture of shared knowledge. Physical contact was necessary—even if it was violent. We all need to be touched.

Almost all the social occasions on the street were accompanied by heavy drinking. Almost all the humor was at the expense of someone else. The streetwise seemed to enjoy mercilessly picking on people they called "do-gooders." I recalled a time in the park in Raleigh when Jay and the other men had talked about a couple of people who'd been giving out articles of clothing. The men went on for hours about the do-gooders appearance, what they said, how they looked, etc.

One day in Raleigh when Jay and I and several others were washing our feet in the fountain a young man came by to evangelize us. He reminded us that it was Sunday and Jesus had washed the feet of his apostles to remind us that we must serve each other. While he was making his point, Jay began to cough. One by one around the fountain, the others took up the coughing. The young man continued to talk, so Jay began a round of splashing the water. The young man was the focus of the "baptism." He got soaked. As he walked away I thought what strength it took to work with any group.

To work with the people on the street took a huge sense of street humor. It made me feel pretty awful. It wasn't that the street people were unwilling to listen though. I believe these men were just tired of being treated with condescension.

Safe in my hotel room, I had these thoughts for a while, then my eyes would shut and I'd be asleep again. After many of these episodes, I woke up to find that my writing pad was under my head and I still gripped the pencil in my right hand! This time I finally felt rested. I crawled from the bed, went into the shower and once again renewed myself in the warm water. I'd slept away most of the day and I was hungry. It was already late afternoon and I wanted food!

I left my burdensome pack on my bed and went outside into the light and warmth of the day. I looked for something other than fast food. Finding a small café, I ate my fill.

Emerging from the café, I looked down the street and saw a group of men lined up on the sidewalk. I took a little walk in the direction of the men and saw they were waiting outside the St.

Vincent de Paul dining room. I joined a small, quiet group of men and waited with them.

A woman came outside to where we were standing and asked: "Who's here for the meal?"

We all looked at each other. One man near me, made a rather rude comment, the woman laughed, and ushered us all inside.

I sat at the table next to the rude man. "Can you believe the questions of some people?" he said. "Here we are in a line to get something to eat. No one else on the block, except us. Not even a kid kicking a can or throwing a rock. What does she expect for an answer?"

Not too anxious to spend much time around this man, I didn't linger too long at the table. I gave my meal to the people around me and soon headed on the way back to my hotel for more sleep. On my way down the street, I watched other men come out of the dining room. They scattered into the park in search of a place to sleep. Some had a cup of coffee, others had a bottle of booze. They were settling in for the night.

I decided to take a little detour from the street to my hotel and walked over to one of the men I'd seen in the dining room. He was bent over from years of self-neglect and life on the streets. His eyes were downcast. He seemed sad. Trying to be friendly I started with, "Was the food any good?"

He pulled a bag of tobacco out of his pocket and rolled a cigarette. He lit the cigarette and quietly puffed to get it started.

I thought he hadn't heard me. So again I asked, "Excuse me, did you get enough to eat?"

He acted like he hadn't heard me. I decided not to try a third time and started to walk away. I'd gone only two steps when a voice behind me said, "I don't eat here for my health."

Turning to face him, I asked, "What do you mean by that?"

The man moved a little closer as he answered. "I used to eat in the best restaurants in Memphis. I had a chauffeured car of my own. Then my wife up and left with everything except the pack of cigarettes I had in my shirt pocket."

He was close enough that I could smell his unwashed body. He reached into his shirt pocket as if to reenact the time when his wife left. He gave me a quick glance to see if I was listening. I stared intently into his eyes. He looked down once again.

He stood very still. His face had the vacant look I saw on so many men who'd been on the streets for a long time. He didn't move away from me. I got the impression he wanted to stay. Awkwardly, he asked, "If you want you can sit next to me when they open the doors at the soup kitchen tomorrow and we can go in together for food."

I was sure this was a major invitation from a man who'd built up a very hard protective shell. I gladly agreed to meet him the next day.

I had one more good night of rest. Getting up early the next day, I headed out to the soup kitchen. I was surprised to see no people waiting in front of the door. In fact the door was closed tight. I knocked loudly.

A woman answered the door. She gave me a quizzical look as I asked, "Sorry to bother you, but aren't you serving breakfast?"

She seemed surprised that I didn't know the schedule. "No," she replied, "We don't open til supper tonight at 5:30. You're welcome to come in for a snack if you're really hungry."

"No, thanks," I said. "I was going to meet a man here for breakfast."

"Okay, bye," she responded and closed the door.

I turned to go and noticed my "friend" was right behind me. His eyes were downcast like the night before. I asked, "Do you want to walk with me for a little while? I'm not too exciting as company, but you're welcome to walk along with me for as long as you like."

I thought I saw a glimmer of a light in his eyes and the faint hint of a smile on his lips. Something in his little smile made me think there was more to this guy than what he appeared to be. I took a chance and said, "Tell me about you."

"Well, I really was rich at one time. I had a string of bad luck after my wife left and I got into some bad stuff. You know what I mean."

Actually I didn't really know what he meant. But I was willing to wait for him to explain. We kept walking.

"You think I'm crazy, don't you?" he demanded.

Without hesitation, I said, "Absolutely not! If you want to tell me what happened, go ahead. If not, don't worry about it."

As I said the words "don't worry," the man abruptly sat down on a bus-stop bench we were passing. I almost tripped over him —we'd been that close. He turned towards me and I took that as an invitation to sit down next to him.

"Why are you so different?" he asked.

"Maybe you're different than you were a few minutes ago," was my answer.

Then he asked me, "Are you afraid of me?"

I hesitated in apparent thought. He looked very serious.

Before I could answer he continued, "I'm a murderer."

Oh, my God, I thought, here we go again. What have I gotten myself into? He's probably stalking me like the person he killed. Maybe worse. Maybe he's already made up his mind to kill me and is just waiting for an opportunity. Either way, if this is my time, it's my time. In spite of my inner reaction to his words, I decided I'd take a chance and continue the conversation. Maybe this was just a fantasy story.

He sat and looked at me. When his eyes met mine, I wasn't really frightened. I wanted to give him a chance to tell me his story. I asked, "Who did you murder?"

His answer was so muffled I couldn't understand him. So I said, "I'm sorry, I didn't catch what you just said. Would you speak up so I can hear you a little easier?"

The man said, "Myself, I killed myself when my wife left." His eyes reddened as tears welled up. His lower lip quivered and his head slumped even further down between his shoulders. "I killed myself when my wife left," he repeated. "Do you understand?"

I took a wild stab at understanding. Mustering up all the compassion I could find inside, I said, "I know that if I lost my wife that a little bit of me would die as well. Is that what you mean?"

"Yes! You understand!" He reached into his pocket and took out a very soiled Taco Bell napkin, blew his nose and wiped his eyes. "Why doesn't anyone understand me when I tell them I killed myself?"

I spoke with a great deal of relief and newfound confidence when I replied, "Too many people have their own problems to..."

He interrupted, "That's it! That's it exactly." He began to get excited. There was a huge smile on his face as he rose from the bench and walked away with a noticeable new bounce in his step.

Wow, I thought. What amazing things happen when people listen to each other. I looked for him that night at the soup kitchen. He never showed up. I wondered if his exuberance had lasted very long. I'd never know. People came and went on these streets. There were not too many lasting connections I was making.

Dinner in the dining room consisted of grits, pork rinds and collard greens. I left feeling full and ready for one last good night's rest at the motel. I went to my room and retrieved the pencil and my journal and headed outside again to find a restful place to write. No sooner did I exit the motel door to the street than I spied my "friend" with the downcast head. He seemed to be peeking at me from around the corner of the building.

"Hi. You startled me," I said. "Wannna walk with me to the park. I'm heading over there to write down a few of my thoughts."

This wasn't the same man I'd seen that morning. "I forgot to tell you who I am," he stated. "My name is Phil. I forgot to tell you that and I forgot to shake your hand too."

Startled by his outstretched hand I reached out to grip it. "People call me Old Man," I said. "I'm really glad to meet you."

We walked together to the park and had a reasonable conversation along the way. We talked about life and faith and people and the goodness of God (one of my favorite topics).

There was a long white pergola next to the riverbank. We aimed for a picnic table where I could sit and write. We settled in and for the next three hours we just sat companionably. I wrote and Phil sat and rolled one cigarette after another. I'd look up occasionally. Once he noticed I was watching him and he offered me a cigarette. I refused and watched as he stuffed another rolled cigarette into an old Marlborough pack. It was pleasant being in each other's company.

Dusk was my favorite time of the evening. With the setting of the sun I liked the slight coolness that enveloped us. We got up from the table and started our walk back toward my motel. Stopping at a fast food joint, we bought each other some coffee.

"I'll buy yours," said Phil.

"Then I'll buy yours," I retorted.

We both laughed. We had some kind of connection.

"You know," he said, fumbling in his pocket for one of the newly rolled cigarettes, "You're an odd one."

I smiled.

He continued, "What you have is what a lot of people are looking for."

Whoa, I thought. Is this the same guy I met yesterday?

"I'm leaving town tonight and I wondered if you'd like to come with me? I'm gonna go home to Wichita Falls where my Mom lives. I haven't seen my family in a long, long time. But now I'm not afraid to go home to see them. I don't know exactly what you said to me, but you got me thinkin' 'bout how I had it when I was living near my Mom. You're a good man. What do you say to coming with me and meetin' my Mom?"

"Oh, Phil," I said. "I can't do that, I have other plans." (I was on my way home too, but I couldn't tell him that.)

"I don't imagine you could change yer plans if I bought you a bus ticket?" he insisted.

We shared a moment of silence as I pondered his offer. Then I shook my head "no" and smiled. I felt like he could get home without my help.

"That's all right," said Phil. His smile and happy demeanor reflected his next comments. "I guess it's time for me to face the music. You remember when I told you earlier that I lost my wife?"

Of course I remembered.

He went on, "I just wanted to let you know—now that you and I are friends—that she left me because of my drinking. I'm on the wagon now, thanks to you, I don't need the juice any more. What do you think about that?"

"Phil, you're doing this whole thing on your own. I just happened to be here at the time you were ready to stop drinking. And I was blessed too to be here when you made the decision to go back home. Don't you see how God has blessed us both? I want you to know that I'll be praying for you as you travel home. You say, I'm a good man? Phil, you are a good man. You have wrestled with the devil and you're still standing! Congratulations!"

We shook hands and once again went in our opposite directions. He headed to the bus station and I headed back to the park. I had to write down these last events—this miracle I'd just witnessed.

CHAPTER 23

Dark finally overcame my efforts to write and I made my way back to the motel. I sank onto the blessed bed and let sleep take over my body and mind.

My first thoughts in the morning were of Phil. Where was he? What was he thinking? How did he feel? My second thoughts took me into the shower where I not only bathed, but I also prayed my own special version of the Rosary that had been a daily ritual on the road. I checked out of the motel and headed for the park with a thank you prayer in my heart. I felt so blessed with the simple little ways God showed his love to me. The songs of birds were everywhere and I thought it couldn't get better than this! What a wonderful way to start the day!

I returned to the pergola next to the river. I pulled out the pencil, paper and my knife that I used as a pencil sharpener. My paper pads were dog eared and soggy from days of being crammed into my backpack. I was at the end of both pads and decided I'd go buy some new writing paper. I wandered the streets of Knoxville for a while, stopping once to buy the paper. Then I headed back toward the less populated areas of the city along the river.

I walked along the riverbank for some time until I encountered a dam made of discarded garbage washed up into a rocky
area. It caused the water to sit and stagnate in a low area of the
riverbank. I stooped down and took some time to clear the debris
and got the water flowing clearly in this one small area. I mar-
veled at the beauty of the flowing water over the rocks, the current and the shapes and colors of objects washed in the water.

Heading away from the riverbank I arrived at the railroad
yard. I was surprised at how close it was to the park I'd just left. I
hadn't really noticed the sound of trains in previous days. It
seemed like a far away time when Phil had told me he would go
home.

Next to the rail yard was a small café. It reminded me of the
little one in Oregon when I had met Edna and May. I stood in
front of the café savoring the sights and sounds. The smell of good
food mixed with the smell of diesel fuel permeated my senses. I
watched the trains slowly chugging in and out of the train yard
and fantasized about hitching a ride on one of them and about all
the places it would take me. Then I turned and entered the diner
and promptly forgot about riding trains.

The menu was brief and simple. Most of it seemed appealing
except the lettuce and onion pie! I had grim childhood memories
of lettuce and onion pie. We'd been poor and my mother had
tried to feed us as best she could. But I was never a fan of lettuce
and onion pie.

I had a good meal and walked out of the diner quite satisfied.
The sky outside was amazing! There were a few clouds and I could
smell a faint hint of rain. I kept repeating to myself "Life is good."
Even though the recent obstacles had been ponderous at times, I
refused to see it any other way. "Life is good" continued to be my
mantra as I longed to be in the loving arms of my wife.

Walking harder and faster than I had in weeks, I soon discovered that I had a hitchhiking rock in my left shoe. My young

friends back home, Mike and Laura had given me a new pair of shoes before I left on my trip. I'd stuck them in my backpack and carried them until my first pair of shoes just wore out. I was wearing the Mike and Laura shoes now and as I stopped and took out the offending rock I had very warm thoughts of these two young people. They were two among hundreds of teens who I'd been privileged to accompany on our trips to Mexico and Arizona. We'd had some incredible times together working with poor and disenfranchised peoples.

I lay down that night in a place alongside of the road. Again I found shelter in the bushes and trees—any place where I could be invisible. I fell asleep praying my thanks to God for all His gifts to me.

Morning came quickly. I woke up slightly disoriented from a pretty hard night's rest on the ground. I'd been dreaming. Finally, I was dreaming again.

In my dream I was lifted off the ground and floating over the river where I'd released the trash the previous day. My wife, Sue, was by my side. My voice in the dream asked: "Which road should I take?" and the answer came "West!"

This was definite confirmation to me of my decision to go home.

As I became fully awake, I wrote this message down on a piece of paper—it was so precious to me. I then decided to lighten my load for the long road home.

I dumped out my backpack onto the ground (not unlike what I'd had to do for the policeman on Highway 95). I ordered myself to look at this mess and see how I could lighten my load—what did I really need versus what did I want? The first thing to go was a pair of socks with holes in the toes the size of light bulbs. I made two piles—a "keep" pile and a "discard" pile. As I examined each item, I relived my journey of the past weeks. When I was finished,

I neatly packed my backpack—much lighter now—and also neatly bundled my discards and placed them next to a sleeping man in a small nearby homeless encampment.

I once again set off on my two tired legs hoping this would be a good day to get a ride. Before I'd gone very far I heard the sound of a train whistle. I turned and saw a cloud of black smoke belching out of a diesel engine that was just coming around the bend in the tracks. The whistle had also awakened the encampment of sleeping men that were still within my view. I could see the man looking at the pile I'd left near him. I watched as he dived into the bundle—his excitement visible to me from where I stood. I felt like Santa Claus.

For a moment, when my attention returned to the train crawling by, I was tempted to hop on. I'd need to get a good running start. As I studied the situation I could see there were too many trains going by on too many tracks—I was going to have to give up on this dream. Besides, walking was glorious and peaceful.

I was a little hungry, but felt refreshed and happy. I was on my feet and on my way west. In my excitement the issues of being homeless seemed to fade.

I was a little concerned about the money I had spent. When I'd dumped my pack, I hadn't found as much as I thought I had. I knew I had spent some, but apparently I had also lost some. I figured I could get work along the way if I ran out. After all I did have 2300 miles to go. I didn't know how long it might take....

Walking through the morning the heat began to build. The sweat poured down my face. I didn't notice the heat or the sweat because I was absorbed in thankfulness for being alive, being able to see the shadowy details of my surroundings, being able to walk. I was overwhelmed with gratefulness for this journey and the people I'd met. I was excited about what lay ahead. My muscles ached but they were working to get me back home.

I thought of the old man on the steps of Saint John the Baptist Church in Savannah. Somehow the memory of him gave me renewed strength to walk with longer strides. My thoughts tumbled over each other. A new clarity about God and my position in creation began to take form. The realization that we are all one in God hit me again and again. With no distance between God's love and me, the physical distance between me and my love, Sue, was insignificant. I walked on peacefully in the warm Tennessee sun. The aching in my joints and the still blurred vision could not dampen my spirit. I was truly the most blessed man on earth.

One foot in front of the other became a march. The ground peeled away as though each step was a page turning toward the conclusion of a very good book that I didn't want to end. As much as I missed my family this moment became my personal precious present.

The veil of fog I'd been living in seemed to have parted as I walked on my way home. The child I'd been instructed to be by the wise old man on the steps in Savannah was erupting from my spirit. As I walked I asked God to come out and play—just as a child would ask his daddy.

I felt God's gift of unconditional love as I skipped along over the grass. "Take off your shoes, Little One," I heard inside my head. I plunked down on the grass and quickly removed my shoes and my backpack. I was laughing and singing at the same time. I tried to turn a cartwheel. Bam! I hit the ground! (I must have been quite a sight.)

My feeling of freedom was amazing. I wished everyone could experience this. I thought it must be something like the feeling that attacked Ebenezer Scrooge in "A Christmas Carol."

"God's love is amazing," I thought to myself as I continued my walk—spitting out the grass from several unsuccessful cartwheel attempts. I was completely wrapped in this awareness that God loves me! And, I thought, all we have to do is ask—"Daddy,

I'm here, come find me." I could die a happy man. I guessed the only reason I did not die was because God was not finished with me yet.

As I walked I thought—and thought. Maybe I'd finally gone crazy! Well, if this was crazy then I'd like to keep it—wrap it up like the gift it was and take it with me every day in every way. The day wandered on as I did. The feelings of bliss stayed with me. This was the best day I'd had.

My thoughts began to slow. I stopped and pulled out my water bottle and took a long thirsty swill. A realization hit me: evil is avoidable, God is not. My thoughts stopped. I sat on the side of the road and waited. I tried to just listen to the voice inside me.

I wasn't at all sure what was happening to me. The light from the west was intense and I had to squint and keep my head lowered to prevent my eyes from rebelling. I kept sitting there until the sun dipped below the trees. Once again I could see Highway 40 stretching out before me. For the first time since the morning, I put on my shoes. It was as though I'd had to experience this day from the very soles of my feet with complete openness to whatever the day would reveal. I began to walk again with a new spring in my step and my new mantra fueling me: evil is avoidable, God is not.

I thought about how I could share this message with others. How it could help people be kind to each other. But what if people didn't pay attention to this message. Then I'd think I just had to stop thinking. Once again I'd walk along, unhurried and unconcerned, but happy.

By now, the daylight was spent. Cars whizzing by seemed to be sending a message of hurry and worry felt by the rest of the world, but not me. I had hoped someone would give me a ride. It didn't seem as though that was in the plan. Perhaps the night had other plans for me, just as the day had.

A tall pine tree offered a cozy place to sit down and write some of my adventures—before I forgot any of the day's events. I found my light, pencil and the crusty writing pad and began to write. Before I knew it I was waking up still holding the pencil in my hand. I had slept deeply and was slightly disoriented. I looked at my watch and saw only one hour had passed. I felt refreshed and began again to write: So much life passes in such a short amount of time it's hard to put all that happens and all that I believe on one piece of paper. I wrote for a long time, oblivious to my surroundings.

Lots of noise and activity broke my concentration. I realized I was sitting near a truck stop. Tons of big rigs were nearby and some were even headed into the rest area where I was sitting. They were all heading west!

I finished writing and removed myself into the trees where I was away from the truck noise. I was exhausted! I lay in the trees looking up and listening to the crickets and June bugs. I felt very relaxed. I wanted to sleep, but my earlier nap seemed to be keeping me awake.

I thought about how all I wanted to do was whatever was God's will for me. I wanted to trust and to love—unconditionally. I wanted to say "yes" to God. My only question was: How?

Sometime near dawn I did fall asleep.

I dreamed of a foggy outline of people moving like dancing shadows. The scene was beautiful and sad—at the same time. The lines and colors seemed as natural as the colors on a painter's palette. The lines and colors blended into each other just like they had when I'd been blind in the bush. If the dream had been a painting it would have made no sense—it had no scheme in its composition—but it was just a dream. Somehow because I had been blind, the blending of colors was understandable to me. It made me happy. For some reason the dream made me feel closer to my family.

When I awakened I felt even more committed to going home.

My dream reminded me of times I had challenged other people to live on the edge—try things that made them uncomfortable. I was in the habit of taking people with me when I fed the Mexican workers who waited on the street for day work. Or when I'd encourage people to invite a homeless person to lunch with them. Many of my friends had accompanied me to Tijuana, Mexico where we often scooped up street children, took them to the park, played with them and fed them.

I thought about my desire to be one with the heart of the homeless. It was happening. I wondered how I could explain this to my family. I hoped they could understand my need to make this journey.

Getting up from my sleeping place, I made my way to the truck stop. The rest room was pretty dirty, but I put my backpack on the floor and used the mirror above the sink to help me shave. Several men came in and on their way out I could hear their not-so-subtle comments about "some people think these rest stops are private bathrooms." Then a man came in whistling. I joined in the melody as I finished shaving. I left feeling cleaner and ready to find a ride west.

I approached several trucks and got several different responses from the drivers of the big rigs. Several people said, "No, sorry." Others kept their windows rolled up. Some threatened to call the cops and some simply said, "Can't you ask someone else?" One man plainly told me to "get my a__ off his running board!" Finally I heard, "Where are you going?"

"Just about anywhere west," was my hopeful reply.

I enjoyed this man's kindness for about a hundred miles to the outskirts of a town called Cooksville. Herm, the driver, made a point of telling me that hitchhiking was against the law. "You may want to take a few back roads off the interstate. Keep moving so you won't get busted. There's a lot of cops in Tennessee and they'll give you a real hard time if you stick to the main highway. They can get pretty rough with strangers."

I took Herm's advice and took one short ride after another on the back roads. After a couple of days I'd traveled about 400 miles in various types of trucks and other vehicles. Some of the night rides definitely helped to keep the drivers awake. In the daylight I could see what beautiful country this was. Every stop could have been a photo opportunity. I wondered about the history of this part of the country. I passed signs announcing places like Farragut, Rockwood, Crossville, Montgomery and Lebanon. Finally we came to a name I recognized—Nashville, Tennessee.

Just east of Nashville I was left off at a place called Percy Priest Lake. There was a small rest area nestled among tall green trees and an incredibly beautiful lake as a centerpiece. The lakeshore was grassy and there were mounds of rolled up hay every five hundred feet or so along the shore. This happened to be a Sunday morning and I reveled in God's creation. I had to push hard to get myself moving out of this area.

I approached a trucker—he was a big old guy! He said, "I don't normally pick up hitchhikers, but I guess you just got lucky."

We both climbed into the cab of his truck as the rain began to fall once again. The man introduced himself to me as Tex. He took a long drag on his cigarette and invited me to eat anything I'd like of the food he had in the cab. I could see this was a man with a big heart.

"You are going west, aren't you?" I asked.

"Yeah," he said. "I'm going all the way to Memphis."

While Tex finished his cigarette we watched the rainfall. The water was running into the creek by the side of the road. I realized I needed to use the restroom before we drove the approximately 250 miles to Memphis. I asked Tex to wait while I went back inside the building. When I went to wash my hands, I looked down and saw a wallet on the floor by my right foot. "Is this your wallet?" I asked the man next to me.

He glared at me as though I was trying to con him and muttered, "It ain't mine."

Once he'd left, I opened the wallet, found an ID card and realized it belonged to Tex (whose real name appeared to be Eugene).

I walked back to the truck. Shaking off the plastic bag that acted as my rain poncho, I climbed back into the truck cab. I said, "Thanks for waiting." I held out the wallet. "I'll bet you'll be glad to see this."

He looked at me for a long moment. "Thanks," he said. "Remember, my name's Tex, not Eugene. What's yours?"

"Oh, people just call me Old Man."

"You don't much like your name either?" he said with a smile.

"I'd just as soon be known as Old Man if you don't mind. That's good enough."

Names and identities settled, Tex then said he'd like to do something nice for me in return for the discovery of his wallet. I assured him that getting me to Memphis was the best gift he could give me. As I buckled my seatbelt Tex asked, "Are you a Christian?"

"Yes, sir, I'm working on it. How about you Tex?"

Tex took his time (a long time) answering the question. I was a captive audience, so I listened.

"My wife tried to make me into a Christian once, but she died before she could do it. I'm a Vietnam vet. I met my wife when I was on furlough in Fort Worth, Texas. There was a dance in the USO and her best friend, Gloria, introduced Sarah and me. I was nineteen and she was twenty-two. Gloria was my date that night and I really tried to be a gentleman and show her a good time. But truthfully, I couldn't think of anyone but Sarah after we met. I found our later that Gloria had really wanted me to meet Sarah, cause she thought we'd make a great match.

The minute I laid eyes on Sarah I knew she was the one for me. Eighteen months later we got married."

It was about this time in his narrative, that I lost track of what he was saying and started to daydream about how my wife and I had met. Her best friend, Julie, had introduced us and it was love at first sight and we got married eighteen months later! The similarities were startling.

I resumed listening to Tex as he was saying: "Sarah kept her job in Dallas as a dental technician and I was discharged from the Army. With my experience in the Army motor pool, I got a job with JB Hunt driving split loads to Nashville. We were married twenty-two years and had six kids—four boys and two girls. My youngest two are still with me. The rest of the kids are married and have kids of their own."

I tried to listen intently and not interrupt, but our lives were eerily similar. Sue and I have had six kids: four boys and two girls —though one of our daughters had died at birth.

Tex continued, "My wife died in 1994 of cancer. It tore me apart. Our family came together like never before. We were always close, but not like this." He stopped to choke back tears. Then he went on, "My kids were so good about the support they gave me. Sarah's mom and dad wanted to move in with us. But we all decided together to let life move along on it's own pace. What else could I do? Some of my relatives and Sarah's mom wanted me to become a Christian by getting baptized and joining their church. I knew that wasn't for me. That's not how I worship God. I've always seen God and me as friends. God is with me wherever I am. I don't need a church to remind me of God's friendship."

As Tex finished his explanation, I turned to look out the window into the dark. I took a deep breath and Tex muttered, "I don't know why I'm telling you all this stuff, I don't even talk to my in-laws this much about Sarah."

I smiled and reached my hand over to his shoulder. "You're a brave man, Tex. You probably just needed someone you don't know to share this tragedy with."

"Well, it looks like I picked the right guy to travel with tonight."

"Thanks. You seem to have a good grasp of who God is to you. So many people I know haven't allowed God to get that close to them."

For the next several hours we talked about God and life and marriage and family. We were both enjoying each other and really didn't want this to end. But the time came for him to let me out. He said, "This is a good spot to get a ride."

I responded, "Maybe we'll meet up again someday and we can pick up where we left off." We both knew that would not happen.

I waived goodbye with a sense of sadness. I knew I was leaving another friend who I would never see again.

CHAPTER 24

I began to strategize about getting
another ride. I realized I smelled pretty bad. I'd had several rides
recently that hadn't lasted very long—I thought my body odor
might have been part of the problem. So I looked around for a
place where I could get cleaned up.

I saw a McDonald's nearby and headed toward it. I used the
restroom to get as clean as I could and then bought a hot cup of
coffee. The coffee and I found a safe place under a tree not too far
from the highway. I sat down to rest and promptly fell into a
dreamy sleep.

*I dreamed I was leaning back on one elbow, drinking my warm cup
of coffee. I heard music coming from a nearby building and the sounds
of children playing. It seemed like my younger days as a musician. I lay
in the arms of my wife, with my children playing hide and seek on top of
a grassy knoll.*

*"I see you, you're it!" they shouted to one another as they ran
down to a flat grassy area.*

I drank in the warm, refreshing morning air.

I felt a deep snore then I woke up with a jerk! I thought, "My children are all grown. Where am I?" My eyes opened to the world as it had been before I fell asleep. I really wanted to just roll over and go back to sleep. The dream had been so pleasant, but that was not to be. I'd spilled the remainder of my coffee when I'd jerked awake. I was having a hard time coming back into the present. It didn't help that my vision was still blurred so that I felt like I was in a dream most of the time.

The night of riding with Tex in the truck turned into another hot day. I walked along the side of the road and thought a lot about the past. My dream had caused me to hunger for those good family times. My back and hips were hurting with every step. I was in the middle of nowhere and I felt a desperate need to get home. I touched my mid section and realized there was a larger roll of fat than when I'd left home. "Wait a minute!" I thought. "I'm supposed to lose weight while being homeless." Whatever had caused my increase in weight; I began to realize that the added pounds were certainly causing me lots more suffering as I walked with the heavy pack on my back. (Later on my wife commented that the food I'd been eating in the soup kitchens was very high in fat and carbohydrates.)

Walking and trying to get a ride were difficult to do at the same time. The rain began again and soon became major showers. I was quickly getting soaked to the skin. Again the depression began to hit me. The sun was going down, the rain was chilling me and I tried to look for some kind of place to get out of the water. Down the road I could see another truck stop.

I thought I wouldn't have too much trouble looking out-of-breath and desperate while asking for a ride. (I'd discovered this technique was very successful.) People generally felt sorry for a person standing in the rain. I was counting on some good-natured person feeling sorry for me. Luckily it worked.

I hopped (as best I could) up into the cab of the truck. The generous driver was quite friendly. But his dog was not. As I sat next to the window, the tiny, very round Chihuahua barked incessantly. The dog had it's own bed behind the passenger seat. As we pulled out into the roadway the barking became even more frantic. The driver told me I was blocking the dog's view. I shifted my position and the barking stopped!

The dog was so pudgy that his legs hardly reached around his belly to the blanket that was underneath him. When the driver turned a corner, the dog kind of rolled to the side—his two legs holding him from rolling over completely. If the driver turned too fast, the dog just rolled and rolled.

The driver seemed delighted to have a passenger. Maybe he thought I was his good deed for the day. He definitely wanted company. He immediately began to talk. It was slightly difficult to carry on a conversation because every time I turned toward the driver I looked into the eyes of the dog and the barking would start up, preceded by great growls! I thought I'd better get to know this dog and asked, "What's his name?"

"That there's Mickey Mouse. He's my guard dog."

I smiled at the thought of this living wiener being a guard dog. I turned again, this time intentionally looking at the dog. This set off about five minutes of barking and growling that would have made a German shepherd feel proud. That episode was the final lesson for me. I would not look at this creature again—not if I could help it!

Over the noise of the nasty little attitude coming from the sleeper I heard the driver tell me his name was Chuck. I told him how nice it was to met him and then introduced myself.

"Don't mind Mickey," Chuck said. "He's a little territorial and he doesn't let up until he's sure you know what belongs to him."

"Oh, how do I show him that I don't want to take his territory away from him?" I asked.

Chuck reached over and gave Mickey Mouse a little scratch behind the ear and said, "Just don't look him in the eye. You'll get along just fine. There is another way to make friends with him. If you want to buy him a beer, he'll drink with you. That's how he got so fat."

I noticed that Chuck looked a little like Mickey Mouse. They were both spreading around the middle and graying around the muzzle. Their tempers were identical. Chuck would yap obscenities at other drivers for any infraction of his perceived territory.

Several hours of driving with these two almost drove me nuts. Mid afternoon we arrived in a rest area near Little Rock, Arkansas. Chuck promptly took Mickey Mouse down from his perch and placed him on the grass. Mickey proceeded to leave a round little brown relic. Chuck picked up the dog and left the treasure on the grass where anyone could step into it. When Chuck went into the restroom, I scooped it up with a paper bag and dumped it into the trash. Then I walked around the lawn, trying to stretch out from the long ride.

When Chuck came back to the truck he asked me if I'd like to continue with him.

"Where are you heading?" I asked.

"I plan to head south towards Dallas."

"That sounds great to me," I replied.

Chuck seemed to like talking to me. I didn't interrupt too much. In fact a lot of the time I was thinking about other things. Chuck shared some pretty private stuff about family. Mickey calmed down and actually began to allow me to smile at him with just the hint of a growl in reply. Chuck started a contest (which he won) to see who could make the longest nonsense sentence that sounded like it made sense. He had a long string of fun and interesting stories. Unfortunately, the tape kept rewinding....

Most stories began with "I love Mickey Mouse because he..." or "My oldest kid was born on a pool table." The ever-vigilant

Mickey would perk up at the beginning of each story (as if he was interested) and as the story progressed, Mickey would lay his head back down on the blanket and fall into a fitful sleep. The hours ground away as one story followed another. Finally the Dallas skyline came into view.

I offered to buy Chuck a steak dinner—for the pleasure of being able to ride with him. He said he just wanted to get home as quickly as possible and declined my invitation. I put on my pack and stepped away from the truck. It was obvious that Mickey wasn't too sad to see me go as he adjusted himself close to the passenger window. He finally had an unobstructed view. I yelled my thanks and Chuck drove off to hearth and home.

It was night again. My eyes were burning. I used the eye drops the doctor had given me, wondering when my eyes would improve. I headed to a wooded area near the rest stop. I wanted to get away from the constant noise of the trucks. My head was buzzing and my mind was racing. So much to think about! I tried to calm myself and began to pray—that always helped. Beyond the woods I found a country road and began to walk.

I realized I didn't know what direction I was walking. The road twisted and turned. I was almost two thousand miles away from home, kind of lost and pretty much broke. I didn't seem to be getting anywhere so I decided to go back to the truck stop. I guessed I'd been walking about an hour when I decided to turn back. On my return to the truck stop, I heard a voice "Hey, friend! Hey you, where ya goin?"

This deep voice was coming to me from the cab of a Peterbilt truck that sat stopped about 25 feet away from me. I headed toward the truck, trying to get close enough for my eyes to see this person.

"Who, me?" I asked.

"Yeah, you. Where ya goin?" the voice asked again.

Now I was close enough to see a round ruddy face that matched the round sounds of his voice. "I'm going out west to California, but I'll go any direction at the moment."

"Well, your sign's upside down."

When I looked quizzically at him, he repeated, "The sign on your pack says south, AND it's upside down!"

"Oh," I said, slightly embarrassed. "Thanks." I pulled off my pack to fix the sign. As I lifted the pack to the ground I was struck again by how heavy it was and now by the smell of it. It smelled like something formerly alive was now dead inside it.

The driver opened the door to the cab and stepped down to the ground. He was a big man—probably weighing in at about 370 pounds! He was wearing a tobacco stained tank top. His belt buckle disappeared under the folds of fat around his middle. A baseball hat was pulled down over his eyebrows, not very successfully containing his thick, dark, bushy hair. He seemed ready to meet a friend. I played along with it. One whiff of the cab of the truck had done a major assault on my nostrils. I knew this was a cab where the aroma of my pack would go virtually unnoticed!

"My name's Harley. I'm going south, like your upside down (ha, ha!) sign says. If you want to ride shotgun, I'll be leavin' in a few minutes. Just have to call my wife from the pay phone over there." He pointed across the parking lot.

"Yeah, that would be great," I said.

"Okay, then, it's settled. See you in a few minutes." And he walked over to the phone.

The odor from Harley's truck permeated every corner of the truck stop. It was apparent he was carrying pigs. I figured that once I got into the cab, the smell would be behind us.

Harley returned from the phone and as we settled into the cab he admonished me to fasten my seat belt. "You'd better buckle up, the police stop us every now and agin."

I followed his orders and then introduced my self as Old Man.

"Yeah," Harley said. "You're Old Man like I'm Harley. Ya runnin' from someone?"

"No, I'm heading home."

"Yeah, California, you said. That right?"

"That's right," I said. "How far you going?"

To my happy surprise he was going to Laredo, Texas. I asked if he'd leave me off in San Antonio where I could get a ride west onto Interstate 10.

"Yeah," he said. His grin showed a number of dark gaps between the yellowed teeth that held his cigar firmly between his lips. "I've been haulin' hogs from Tulsa to Oklahoma City, then on to Laredo for over twenty years now. I love the run and I love the hogs. Hogs don't care what ya smell like, only how ya treat 'em."

I completely understood his analogy. "So how'd you get the name Harley?" I asked.

He had a kind of frontier poetic flourish and began to answer. "Me and my old lady"… He paused for effect, getting into character. "Me and my old lady tried ridin' motorcycles. Bouncin' around with the old lady on the back, it was easy fallin' in love with ridin'. The old lady fell in love with it too. So we chopped a couple of Harley Davidson motorcycles into hard tails. From that time on it was like we were married to our bikes. We was in love with our choppers. I drive real hogs to the market and it kinda reminds me of my "hog" waitin for me at home. I mean my bike, ya know, not my old lady. Ya don' really know what it's like til ya have one and take it out on a ride. Ya know what I mean don'tcha?"

I was with him "Yeah, you have to experience something like riding to understand the feeling of freedom that comes with it. Is that it?"

"Yeah," said Harley with a big squeeze of the cigar between his lips. "Ya got it!"

As I had hoped the smell of the pigs kind of merged with the smell of the backpack. We bounced along companionably, though Harley liked the bouncing way more than me. He enjoyed the stories of the other drivers I'd met on the road. He seemed to feel some connection with others who had exotic names like Tex and Tornado.

He was slightly unpredictable. Once breaking a long run of silence with, "What the hell ya doin', Mister?"

I didn't have a clue what he was talking about. I looked around the truck cab searching for a reason for his outbreak.

"Ya got yer stuff all over the place. Look at cha!" Indeed I had been shuffling through my pack and had placed some of my clothes on the seat beside me.

"Whatcha think this is, a hotel?"

I quickly apologized. Harley said, "Ah, I was jes jokin round."

I wasn't sure how much of his joking was serious. As a gesture of reconciliation Harley offered me some of his chicken soup. "My ol lady made soup for me before I took off. Ya want some?"

I feared being rude so of course I said, "Sure, sounds good Harley."

We rode on in silence. At the end of our journey together we seemed content with the time we had shared. I was grateful for the ride and he seemed glad to have helped someone. He had pointed out a number of my flaws along the road, but had also complimented me "Ya got a lot of guts hitchhiking out here in the south."

We arrived in San Antonio about nine o'clock on a Sunday morning. I got out of the truck and made sure my sign said west and made my way to Burger King. I ordered a chicken sandwich, fries and a coke. The restaurant had a second floor so I took my tray upstairs to sit at a table and rest in peace. I ate and took my time enjoying the view I had of the Alamo from this vantage point. No hurry. No worry. I was on the final leg of my journey home.

I pulled out my journal to write down the events of the past couple of days. As I began to write I noticed a young family who had joined me in the upstairs dining area. There was a mom and baby who waited while the dad went downstairs to get food. He had just left when the baby, a newborn, began to cry. The mother unbuttoned her blouse and pulled the baby toward her. With my fuzzy eyesight, I could see the outline of the young mother and baby. It was a beautiful scene.

I was deep in thought and memories when I looked up at the clock. I had been writing for four hours! The young couple had gone and my concentration was broken with the entrance of a young man. He approached me and presented me with a blue beaded chain and a card that read: "I am deaf. I am selling key chains for $1.00. Smile, these items are for living. God bless you and thank you."

His bravery gave me a second wind. I shuffled my papers and put them in my backpack of ever increasing weight. Leaving Burger King, I wandered the streets of San Antonio. It was a beautiful day. I called Sue—because it was Sunday. She was pleased I was in San Antonio and on my way home.

That evening I used a few of my precious dollars on a run down motel room. I puzzled over where all the money had gone —the money I'd earned from driving and other jobs. I needed a shower and a bed. It seemed like a good use of my dwindling resources.

I did get a good night's sleep and I felt at peace with myself the next morning. I spent the morning walking—no one seemed at all interested in picking me up. I walked and prayed in peace. Today it felt good.

Some distance out of San Antonio, a driver who was on his way to Kerrville, Texas picked me up. We drove for about twenty minutes. He never spoke to me. I mentioned how beautiful the town was.

"Young man," he said, rather facetiously, "maybe you should bring your girlfriend here, she'd probably like it too."

I thought that was a rather odd comment. But he was right— Sue would like this town. Sue would have liked a lot of the towns I'd been through. Maybe someday I could show her some of the places I'd seen—maybe not all the bushes and dumpsters, but certainly the cities and towns and back roads. This is one big and beautiful country.

I was on my way home. Part of me wanted to stay where I was. The other part of me could hardly wait to see my family. All through my adventure, I had written and drawn my experiences. I was excited to share these with people I loved.

I sat down by the side of the road and looked over some of the sketches I'd done. They vividly reminded me of these past weeks on the road. I delved deeper into my pack and discovered the small gifts I'd found along the way had all been destroyed by the water and bad packing—no gifts for the family.

Back to hitchhiking, I made my way through New Mexico and into Phoenix, Arizona. There I met a trucker who said he was going to Las Vegas, Nevada. I liked that idea, besides his cab was air conditioned and very comfortable. The driver, Victor, seemed to be satisfied with life and all it had to offer. He was on his way to gamble the two hundred dollars in his pocket. His lifestyle seemed simple enough: unmarried and ready for an adventure in Las Vegas or any other place that called him.

He mused, "I love driving along the empty highway with my windows down and the smell of the dry desert air. But not when it's this hot! The smell of the desert flowers is subtle—too faint to be perceptible to the untrained nose."

I replied, "Yeah, I love the desert and the smells and all God has to offer."

Victor looked at me. "You're not gonna give me a sermon now, are you?"

I laughed to myself. "There's nothing I do worse than give a sermon. I'm much like you are. Nature is a gift and I enjoy it. I'm glad you do too, Victor."

"Oh, for a minute there I thought you were going on some rampage about how I wasn't saved unless I accepted the Lord, Jesus Christ or something like that."

I could see where this conversation was going. We didn't share the same views on church and church people. I didn't want to scare Victor away from the truth, but I didn't want to be wishy-washy about my faith either. So, I continued, "Every man and woman is entitled to their own belief system. I believe that being good and loving are the messages to follow through on."

Victor seemed satisfied with the explanation of my spirituality. I knew that if I pressed too much more, I might end up outside the truck walking in the beautiful hot desert! Unfortunately the air conditioning gave out shortly after our exchange of views.

"Damn, I need to replace a fuse in the fan. We'll just have to ride with the windows down the rest of the way," Victor announced as he began to roll down his window and let a blast of hot air into the cab.

The desert heat was dry and the sweat evaporated almost as quickly as it formed. I had two bottles of water that we shared. We drove for miles on never ending highways. Nearing Las Vegas Victor exclaimed, "We've been on the road a couple of hours without you mentioning religion, Old Man. We're coming over the rise to 'Sin City' itself. Doesn't that make you want to preach the gospel to me or something?"

I was tired and hot. I didn't know if I wanted to accept this challenge. But we were almost to our destination (I figured I could walk if I had too.) So I thought I'd go for it!

"Thank you for asking that way, Victor. There's lots of pieces missing in this big old puzzle we call life. Maybe you've picked up a few pieces to fit in the puzzle that I haven't been able to find? My faith is based on my personal spirituality, not just someone else's word. I am Catholic by choice and I love the sacraments and the rituals. That doesn't mean you have to believe the same thing I do or even the same way. Life would be lots less exciting without people's different passions for life, wouldn't you say, Victor?"

Victor was obviously waiting for the punch line, but I never gave it to him. I thought it was best for him to be responsible for his own choices. He was already looking ahead to his gambling escapade—I needn't have worried about walking!

Our last twenty minutes together were pleasant. Victor pointed out places of interest including the Statue of Liberty at the New York, New York Casino. He offered to take me gambling —saying he could hook me up with someone who would loan me money. As for him, he was headed for the casinos, the liquor and the women. I told him he could just let me out anywhere along the Strip. I'd find my own way in Las Vegas.

CHAPTER 25

I've always liked Las Vegas. Aside from the fact that I like to gamble, there is something about the place that fascinates me. The minute I was free of the truck I was transfixed by the awesome sights. The lights were dazzling—even in broad daylight. The sounds of the city assaulted me from all sides. The warm desert air was exhilarating in the presence of all the glitz and glitter everywhere I looked. It reminded me of Disneyland at high speed. My senses were reeling and I realized a deep feeling of sickness was creeping through me. Coming from almost two months of being homeless I was deeply struck by the excess of everything.

I dug into my soggy backpack and discovered enough money that I thought I might stay in a motel six. So down the road I trudged, feeling dirty and sweaty and smelly. By the time I found the Motel 6, dusk was settling and even this place was lit up like a Christmas tree.

Handing over my ID (for the first time in a very long time) I realized I was going to have to become Pete again. I knew this would be the last place I'd be staying before I got home. The lady at the desk said, "Thank you Mr. Fullerton, your room will be $33.60. Enjoy your stay."

Ah, I thought to myself, I never thought I would like hearing the name "Mr. Fullerton" so much. I was ready for a hot shower and a phone call to my wife. Then I headed for the soft bed and the remote control for the T.V.

Somewhere in the middle of the night I was awakened by gunfire. The T.V. was on full blast, the remote still in my hand and people on the screen were shooting at each other. I turned off the T.V. and rolled over only to be awakened later by the sounds of a very loud party. Sleep overcame me once more and pretty soon I heard a loud knock and a voice calling "Maid Service."

Whoa! What time was it? Where was I? I called out to the maid to wait a few minutes while I packed my stuff, put on my black pants and white shirt (Which I'd had for job opportunities) and vacated the room. It was 11:00 a.m. and I was in the city that never sleeps. I headed out thinking that I'd be home today for sure!

Just outside the motel room on the street in the blazing light of day, I came upon an elderly gentleman who was obviously out of breath and in pain. "Can I help you?" I said. Before he could answer I continued, "It looks like we should get you inside out of the sun, if that's all right with you?"

The man looked as though he was having a heart attack, but I hoped it was simply that he was dehydrated. He gave me no reply so I asked, "Where are you going, sir?" And then helped him to sit down on a concrete wall.

"Excuse me, excuse me," I asked of several people passing by. Finally a man stopped to help me. "This gentleman seems to be suffering from the heat. Will you help us please?"

The man said he would go inside the nearby casino to ask security to come and help. We waited several minutes, but our helper didn't return. I'd gone and gotten a cup of water and was trying to get the man to take a drink. A few minutes more passed and he began to talk.

He told me he had come to the strip in a limo. The limo driver had let him off a long way from where he wanted to be. (He thought it might be because the limo driver didn't think he had enough money for a big tip.) He'd been walking a while before I found him. He said he was with a senior citizen's group trip from Atlanta. He'd come with a bunch of people he didn't know. I asked where he was staying, but he didn't seem to be able to focus on that. Finally I got him inside the casino and settled at the bar where the very nice bartender gave him another glass of water. He still looked as though he could pass out at any moment.

Trying not to be rude I asked, "Do you have any money?" I was hoping to somehow get him into a cab back to his hotel (wherever that was).

"Hell yes! I came here to gamble, didn't I?" He was definitely set on this trip.

"Let me get some help for you. You just stay here and I'll be right back."

I went to find security people—they were everywhere. I guided one man in uniform to the old guy. "Don't frighten him," I said. "He's been through quite a bit."

"Don't worry, mister, we do this all the time."

Pretty soon they had him settled in front of a video poker game at the bar, having a drink. He was able to answer the security guard's questions, so they determined he was okay to stay. They ushered him to a table so he could get something to eat. He invited me to have lunch with him. I thought, "What the heck, why not?" and sat down to hear his story.

"I'm a lawyer. I worked in Atlanta and retired last year because I was starting to forget things. Now I'm looking for a little excitement before I kick the bucket. I don't practice the law any more. But I do have a good luck pen from when I won my last case. I'd like you to have it. It looks like you saved my life."

With each drink of water and bite of food, my companion became more and more lucid. He reached into his pocket and retrieved a plastic ballpoint pen that had the design of $100 bills imprinted all over its surface. He passed it across the table towards me. "I won't be needing this any more." Then continued, "Where are you headed?"

I thanked him for the pen and told him I was going home. "Today!" I exclaimed. "I can hardly wait to see my family."

"I don't have any family. You're lucky," he said sadly. "There are only a few things I want to do before I die and coming to Las Vegas is one of them."

When I asked if his friends knew where he was, he pretended like he didn't hear me. It seemed like he wasn't going to talk about those kinds of personal things. I wished him well and thanked him for lunch and went outside into the afternoon sun.

It was blisteringly hot. I headed toward a spot on the corner of Highway 15 and Tropicana where Victor had let me out the day before. I thought it would be a great place to get a ride.

I must have been quite the sight with a towel wrapped around my head to protect my bald top from frying. I sat on the corner with my sign saying "west." My shirt was soaked with sweat, my backpack sat at my feet and I was determined to stay here until I had a ride home. So I sat. I could see the roller coaster of New York, New York. It would rise up out of the casino into the sunlight. I envisioned the ticket takers and gamblers in the air-conditioned casino. Probably not one of them was aware of how easily available a drink of water was to them. I was ready to get out of this town.

I sat for hours. People passed by in groups and by themselves. Not one looked at the people passing by them. They certainly didn't notice me! It was like they were holograms—just out of reach of each other. It gave me a really eerie feeling.

I had lots of time to relive the past weeks. What a gift this time had been. I spontaneously began my favorite prayer song: "If you want to live life free, take your time go slowly. Do few things, but do them well. Simple things are holy!" I went on "Thank you God for this time. Thank you for our dream. I tried to do what you asked. Allow me to bring this experience to others. Please forgive me for anything I have missed. I love you! Amen!" Now all I needed was a ride!

Rolls Royces, Bentleys, Masseratis, and Cadillacs passed by. The people inside hidden by tinted glass. Not one car slowed. The hours were endless. The searing sun had set, but it was still very hot. I was desperate for water, but kept vigil at my post—hoping and praying for a ride. I felt paralyzed by heat and dehydration, but I was committed to getting a ride home today. I could not think beyond that. I didn't know what to do. I had no money, not for a meal, not for a hotel, not for a way home.

I stood and stretched and thought I'd look one more time in my backpack to see if that missing money would miraculously show up. Maybe I could find a moldy cliff bar under my damp clothes. Diving into the mess, I felt a lump. There was a little zippered compartment behind my festering belongings at the very bottom of my pack. I unzipped the zipper and pulled out the lump. I stared at the lump in disbelief thinking, "This can't be true!"

The lump was a roll of paper money. I looked closer and saw it was indeed a roll of paper money. I was rich! I shouted out loud, "I'm rich!" I had completely forgotten I'd stashed the money after I'd earned it—keeping it for a "rainy day" so to speak.

The first thing I did was to go to Burger King. I ordered a very tall cold coke. Then I sat down and looked at the money. I began to carefully unwind the bills. They were almost welded to each other from the days in the musty, wet backpack. I separated it into piles. I didn't want to count it all—it seemed like so much. I wanted to be surprised. So I just pulled out $36 and said "Hallelujah, here's the money for another night at Motel 6." What a miracle. I savored the moment when I threw my pack on the bed that had clean sheets and reached to pick up the phone. I called my beloved Sue and told her I'd found some money wadded up in the bottom of my pack. I also told her I'd waited all day for a ride and had not even had one offer.

She asked me to look at how much I had. Then she suggested that I look into getting an airplane ticket.

I hadn't even thought I could do such a thing. I told her I'd call her back after I counted my money and checked the airlines.

My next call home, I told Sue I'd be arriving in San Jose the next day! I was over the top with excitement! I left a message with the front office for a 7:00 a.m. wakeup call and hopped into the shower one more time. I was almost home!

Morning brought another quick shower and shave. I'd taken advantage of the washing machines the night before. I dressed in my clean dress clothes. I tried to look as presentable as I could. I took a taxi to the airport and bought my ticket. Then I sat down to eat breakfast. I started to count my money one last time. Before I could finish counting I heard the call to board the plane. I found my seat, sat down, and strapped my self in. I resumed my counting. I had three tens, six fives, sixteen ones and four dollars in change. Eighty dollars! Exactly the amount I'd started with!

I recalled that in my dream I'd been told, I wouldn't need money. I left home 53 days before with the $80 Sue had insisted I take. My mind was numb with delight. I began to cry. I cried because my adventure was over. I cried because I'd been so blessed by my God. I cried for all the people I'd met, and I cried because I would soon be home in the arms of my love.

Epilogue

Upon my arrival at home I saw the doctor about my eyes. It seemed I had been misdiagnosed. I had some exotic eye infection that would need a couple of years of treatment to keep my sight. As of this date, my sight has returned.

The following summer while in the Arizona desert at our annual summer camp, I was rock climbing with our group near the border of Arizona and Mexico. I was coming down from a perch in the rock and missed my handhold. I plummeted 35 feet to a narrow ledge below, shattering my right ankle in the process. Six weeks later, my right foot was amputated. I would never be able to take such a journey again.

I now have a prosthetic foot that serves me quite well for short walks. I am able to continue my work with the poor in the San Jose area. The summer camp in Arizona is celebrating its 22nd summer this year and is run by dedicated veterans of many Arizona trips.

I am a happy man. I am still able to serve and I have a much better appreciation for the plight of the poor. "What you do to the least of my brethren, you do unto me."

FROM SUE'S PERSPECTIVE

As we began to share Pete's dreams with close family and friends, they would ask me, "What do you think? How do you feel about this?"

I had willingly accepted the dreams as God's calling for Pete. We had decided it would take some time in preparation and 1997 was set as the time for departure. If I was in the least bit stressed about what would happen to him, my stress was relieved on June 13, 1996 when I too had a dream. (You need to know that I never remember my dreams!)

The dream came after Pete had been suffering from a mysterious illness that had caused him to be very disoriented. I'd taken him to the doctor and he'd had tests to see if he was experiencing a stroke or a brain tumor. The tests had showed nothing. I was lying beside him the night of June 13 and I felt like he was going to die. I recall praying fervently to God. I prepared myself to lose him. I consciously let go of him and gave him back to God and then I had this dream.

> I dreamed that Pete and I were lost and I was leading him through a maze of underground spaces. I put him on my back to walk up a very weird set of stairs. I was surprised how easy it was to carry him on my back. Then we were in a strange room and I was looking for a way out. A beautiful blond haired child (who looked amazingly like our (at the time) two-year-old granddaughter, Kayleigh) was in this room. She extended her hand toward us to lead us to safety.

After this dream I knew Pete would be okay.

FROM SUE'S DIARY

August 14, 1997

Today I awoke at 5:00 a.m. in Tim and Lonie's apartment in Ashland, Oregon. I woke Pete at 5:30. He showered and got ready to leave. He walked out the door at 6:15, just as he had wanted. On his way to where?

In the last few days I have wondered why I have so few questions about this "trip" of Pete's. Then I remembered a year ago June, when he was so sick. The night I had the dream I thought he was going to die. I actually prepared myself and let go of him and gave him to God's keeping that night. I now believe God was preparing me for this. I have lit a candle that I will light each night until he returns safely to me.

August 15

Pete called me this morning. He wasn't supposed to call until Sunday, but he was so excited about his first day. He has a job washing dishes!

The kids are calling asking if I've heard anything.

August 16

Tim called this evening—just "checking on Mom." He wasn't at all surprised to hear of Dad's good fortune. He said, "Someone's watching out for him."

As I was going to bed tonight I was thinking of angels. I recalled the little girl in my dream of a year ago. At the time Tim said she was an angel. Tonight it came to me that she is Griffie Terese (our baby daughter that died at birth) who will keep him safe and will lead him where he needs to go.

God go with you my dear. I love you.

August 18

Pete called this am. He met a man who may want him to drive a truck to Denver. He said there was a woman in the restaurant who offered him a place to stay. He declined.

August 19

I am sleeping quite well these days. I burn my candle each evening. Then I go to bed and I'm out!

I am not worried. I just know that he and I are meant to learn some lessons from this time. Lessons yet to be revealed.

August 21
Pete called tonight. He's driving a truck to Denver. He says he's rich! He's getting paid cash—"under the table."

August 22
Pete's been gone a week. It seems like forever.

August 25
Wonder where my dear is tonight?

August 27
Meals for one are sure simple. Tonight I had squash! Wonder where Pete is tonight? I haven't heard from him since Sunday. Alabama?

August 28
Pete called tonight—he just got to Savannah, Georgia. He got a ride with a man trying to get home for the birth of his baby. Pete drove while the man slept—he had come from Texas. Pete was pretty tired too—he'd been hitchhiking for three days and had gotten soaked in the rain.

August 30
I am marveling at how I am surviving without Pete. Of course I miss him, but I know he is returning. I miss him in that space in the bed, but the days are going fast.

It seems like he is having an amazing time.

August 31
Pete called this am. He is still in Savannah. He has stayed in a couple of shelters and says the food is really good.

Peter kind of rolls his eyes when I talked about his father sleeping in a doorway last night.

Pete sounds happy. It was raining as we were talking. He's lost most of his early drawings because they got wet.

September 1
Princess Diana died today. She had really made a decision to live her life and use her influence to help others.

September 3
I continue to light my candle and remind God to take care of my dear.

September 5

Pete called this am from Raleigh, North Carolina. He said it's taken him about four days and lots of walking to get from Savannah to Raleigh. He's not sure what day it is. His sleeping bag is all wet. He is going to try to find a creek to bathe in and a dry place to lay out his sleeping bag.

He doesn't seem to know how long he's been out. Sounds like he's concerned about getting home. Rides are hard to come by.

Julie had the ultrasound—it's a boy!

Mother Theresa died today.

September 7

Pete called this morning. He's sounding really tired. Not quite so excited. It sounds like he's had a difficult few days.

September 10

I have been thinking about Pete all day.

September 13

Pete called today. He is still in Raleigh. He has an eye infection.

September 14

Everyone is asking where Pete is.

September 18

Pete called this morning from Tennessee. He sounded so discouraged. I think if I had told him I wanted him to come home, he would have come. Instead I asked him if he wanted to come home and he said "No." He thought there was more he needs to learn.

He's had lots of alone time. I've had none. Our children are here a lot, I'm working. There's always something to do.

Andy is leaving on his trip across the country on Saturday. This will be the first time in 32 years that I will be living alone!

September 20

Andy came to school today to have lunch with me before he takes off.

Thinking about Pete and our life together and how much we give each other. This separation is easy because I know he's coming home.

September 22
Pete called from Knoxville, Tennessee. He's heading west. I think he's relieved to be heading home.

Andy (our youngest son and the only one left at home) finally left on his road trip. I am alone!

September 26
Pete called from Arkansas, I think. He says he'll be in San Antonio tomorrow. He wants to be home.

Lots of thoughts about what Pete's trip means to us. Where do we go from here?

This is the first time in my life I have lived alone. I've discovered I like to cook and eat, listen to music, pray, read and watch sappy movies. But I still have the best feeling when I do something for someone else.

September 28
What will Pete bring back from his trip? Where is God leading us? I really don't know. I just keep praying to be open to God's call. What is the next step?

October 2
I've been dealing with people coming to the door at home asking to leave things for Truck of Love. Someone filled the trailer with junk that I had to pay $100 to get carted away.

Pete really does lighten my otherwise heavy world. Isn't God wonderful? Who would guess that He would pair us up!

October 5
Pete is coming home! He's getting on a plane in Las Vegas.

Today is Peter's 25th birthday.

I need to get up early in the morning and wash the sheets and clean the bathrooms. It's really hard to believe that this part of the journey is over. What now?

October 9
Pete got home Monday.